Thomas Davis Le

IRISH SAG

IRISH SAGAS

Edited by
MYLES DILLON

The Thomas Davis Lecture Series

Published in collaboration with
Radio Telefís Éireann
by
THE MERCIER PRESS
DUBLIN and CORK

© *The Mercier Press 1968*
Fourth Edition 1985

British Library Cataloguing in Publication Data

Irish sagas.
  1. Tales — Ireland
  I. Dillon, Myles
  398.2'1'09415   GR153.5

ISBN 0-85342-736-4

Printed by Litho Press Co., Midleton, Co. Cork.

CONTENTS

Every autumn, winter, and spring since September 1953, Radio Éireann has been broadcasting half-hour lectures, named in honour of Thomas Davis. Inspired by one of his famous sayings, 'Educate that you may be free,' the aim of these lectures has been to provide in popular form what is best in Irish scholarship and the sciences.

Most of the lectures have been in series; many have been single broadcasts; some have been in English, some in Irish. In the comparatively short time that has passed since they were initiated, the lectures have dealt with many aspects and with many centuries of Irish social life, history, science and literature. The lecturers, distinguished for their special learning at home and abroad, have been drawn from many nations but mainly from Ireland.

INTRODUCTION

In Ireland, as in Wales, poetry and legend are the substance of the literature, and these lectures were meant to serve as an introduction to the prose tales. The stories have a general interest as being based on oral tradition, and preserving at the same time very old material. Ever since the famous archaeologist, Schliemann, proved that Homer was true, so to speak, it has been recognised that traditional singers can preserve evidence of manners and customs from a distant past, and a great deal of research has been done in recent years into the nature of their achievement, the 'creative memory' which they employ. Milman Parry, an American, studied the oral traditions of Yugoslavia, and his pupil A.B. Lord, author of *The Singer of Tales*, and G.S. Kirk of Cambridge, with his *Songs of Homer*, have carried the investigation further. All this lends added interest to the Irish heroic sagas. They too preserve, amid much that is pure fancy, the picture of an old Celtic society such as the ancient historians described as existing in Gaul. Julius Caesar and Strabo and others have described the habits of the Gauls at a feast, their weapons and manner of fighting on the battlefield, and the poetry of their bards. And much of what they tell us is told again in the old Irish manuscripts which preserve the Irish sagas, although these sagas are not earlier than the eighth century.

For example one historian says of the Gauls: 'In former times, when the hind-quarters were served (at a feast), the bravest hero took the thigh-piece, and if another man claimed it, they stood up and fought in

single combat to the death.' This practice is vividly recorded in *The Story of Mac Da Thó's Pig* (p. 79). It
is the principal theme of the great saga *Bricriu's Feast,*
the motif of the Champion's Portion (*curad-mír*), which
is won, of course, by Cú Chulainn, the Irish Achilles
(p. 61).

Another passage is of special interest from this point
of view. It is an account of the Celts of Gaul in battle:
'For their journeys and in battle they use two-horse
chariots, the chariot carrying both charioteer and chief-
tain. When they meet with cavalry in the battle, they
cast their javelins at the enemy, and then descending
from the chariot, join battle with their swords... They
cut off the heads of enemies slain in battle, and attach
them to the necks of their horses.' In *Táin Bó Cúailnge*,
the central saga of the Ulster Cycle, Cú Chulainn, with
Loeg his charioteer, in his two-horse chariot, armed with
spear and sword and shield, is a Celtic warrior just
such as Posidonius describes. And in Ireland too the
taking of the heads of the slain was the custom.

There are four cycles of Irish sagas: the Mythological
Cycle, which consists of a few stories about the gods of
pre-Christian Ireland; the Ulster Cycle, heroic tales
about the Ulster warriors, among whom Cú Chulainn
is the central figure; the Fenian Cycle, tales (and ballads) about a band of warriors (*fian*), from which the
cycle is named; and lastly a cycle of sagas about the
kings of ancient Ireland, many of them historical persons who here have become legendary, rather as have
the heroes of the *Chansons de Geste.*

The Mythological Cycle tells about the Irish Otherworld, the Celtic magic that delighted Matthew Arnold.
It is this Celtic Otherworld that is thought to have inspired the French romances about the Holy Grail.

The Irish Otherworld is a country where there is no sickness nor age nor death; where happiness lasts for ever, food and drink do not diminish when consumed, to wish for something is to possess it; where a hundred years are as one day. This Land of the Living is in the Western sea. A beautiful girl approaches the hero and sings to him of this happy island. He follows her and they sail away in a boat of glass and are seen no more. Or else he returns after three days to find that he has been away for three hundred years. Sometimes it is a castle in which the hero has some strange adventure, and then the castle vanishes, and he finds himself alone again.

One famous tale, not included here, is *The Adventure of Bran* (eighth century). A woman in strange attire appears in Bran's house, and sings to him of the beauty and pleasures of the Otherworld. There is an island supported by pillars of gold. There are chariot-races and boat-races. Lovely colours shine on every side. Joy is constant. Music sounds always in the air. The sea washes the waves against the land so that tresses of crystal fall on the shore. The chariots are of gold and silver and bronze, the horses chestnut, golden, even blue as the sky. The sun-god is described:

'A fair-haired man comes at sun-rise to light up the plain. He rides over the bright land against which the ocean murmurs. He stirs the sea into blood.'

Bran sets out in quest of this happy land with twenty-seven companions. After many wonderful adventures which I cannot now relate, he returns home and finds people assembled on the shore who ask his name. When he says 'I am Bran son of Febal,' they reply: 'We know him not, but the Voyage of Bran is one of our ancient stories.' Bran sailed away, and from that time forward his adventures are not known.

The Ulster Cycle has for its central story *The Cattle-Raid of Cooley (Táin Bó Cúailnge)* with Cú Chulainn as the hero (p. 93). He comes into battle in his chariot, and stands alone at a river-ford defending Ulster in single combat against the Connacht champions. (Single combat is another custom of Gaulish warriors.) There is some history behind this saga, for we know that the Ulaid and the Connachta were enemies. In fact the Ulstermen were defeated. But the saga makes Ulster win, and makes Cú Chulainn triumphant.

Some stories of this cycle are presented as prefatory to the *Táin*, in that they describe events which lead up to the great battle. Of these the most famous, and the best, is *The Exile of the Sons of Uisnech* (p. 53). It is a love-story, the oldest love-story in medieval literature; and this love is irresistible, lasting until death, love which brings the lovers to their doom. It is believed by many scholars to represent the Celtic source of 'Tristan and Iseult', probably the greatest contribution of the Celts to literature.

There is one other Ulster tale which deserves mention, for it is not included in the book, and has in its restraint something of what Claudel, speaking of the Noh plays of Japan, called 'eloquent silence'. It is the story of a father who kills his own son, the motif of the *Hildebrandslied*, and of the Persian tale of Sohrab and Rustum.

Aoife was a woman-warrior in the east, by whom Cú Chulainn had a son. When leaving her, he said that the boy must never tell his name to a single warrior (only to more than one). Years later when the Ulster warriors are assembled by the sea, a little boy comes in over the waves in a boat of bronze with golden oars. One after another the warriors go down to challenge him and are defeated. Then Cú Chulainn goes, in spite of his wife's foreboding. The boy will not tell his name even to Cú Chulainn. They fight with swords and the boy shaves Cú Chulainn's head with his sword. They wrestle in the sea, and the boy puts Cú Chulainn under twice. Then Cú Chulainn resorts to his terrible weapon, the *gae bolga*, a spear with many points which travels over the water, and he kills the boy. As he is dying, the boy calls out the name of a woman in the east from whom Cú Chulainn learned to use the *gae bolga*, and he knows that it is his son. 'It is true,' said Cú Chulainn. He took the boy in his arms, and carried him up and cast him before the Ulstermen. 'Here is my son for you, men of Ulster!' said he.

The Fenian Cycle is not heroic saga at all, but rather the remains of a lost mythology, of which the Celtic god Lug was the central figure. Gerard Murphy showed that Find and Lug are different names of the same god. The *Colloquy of the Old Men* is obviously the work of a single author and has a peculiar charm (p. 119).

The two tales of the Historical Cycle that are discussed here illustrate the scope and nature of these stories. The first is pure legend, the wonderful birth of Cormac, and his accession to the kingship by means of his uttering a true judgement (p. 148) Cormac is not an historical person, and O'Rahilly thought him to be an avatar of Lug (EIHM 284). Our second story (p. 162) employs the motif of Joseph and Potiphar's wife, and of Phaedra and Hippolytus; but Rónán, king of Leinster, is an historical person who lived in the seventh century.

So much for the content of Irish saga. A few words may be said about the form, which is of particular interest. The oldest narrative form known to Indo-

Europeans seems to have been a prose tale with verse dialogue, the verse being fixed and unchanging, the prose left to the creative memory of the story-teller. This was the old Indian form. It is the Irish form. The sagas are in prose. But when the champions are claiming the hero's portion in *The Story of Mac Da Thó's Pig*, they salute each other in verse; when the child Deirdre is born, the druid prophesies in verse; when Deirdre bids farewell to Scotland, and when she laments the death of her lover, she speaks in verse. In India and in Greece, this ancient form gave way to epic poetry, so that we have in the *Mahābhārata* and in the Homeric poems long narratives in verse. But in Ireland the ancient Indo-European form survived down to the Middle Ages, illustrating what can be shown in various other ways, the great archaism of Irish tradition.

M. D.

I

TOCHMARC ÉTAÍNE

By Myles Dillon

We shall tell you in this series of Davis Lectures about Irish heroic literature, that is, about the old Irish sagas. They are indeed the most important part of early Irish prose literature, for we have no historians before Keating and Michael O'Clery, no orators, no dramatists, and the novel is a modern invention. We have plenty of poetry of various kinds, and we have tales about visions of the Otherworld and about voyages in search of the Land of Youth, and we have the sagas. Poetry and legend are the substance of Irish literature.

The sagas fall into four cycles of tales: the Mythological Cycle, the Ulster Cycle, The Fenian Cycle and the Historical Cycle (or Cycles of the Kings, for there are a number of separate cycles with one or other of the early kings as its central figure). You shall hear where these tales are preserved and what they are about, and you shall hear a few of the sagas from each of the four cycles.

The oldest Irish manuscripts are in Latin and are copies of the Psalms and of the Gospels. The earliest of these Irish Latin manuscripts in existence is the Cathach of St. Columba, written towards the end of the sixth century. The Irish sagas are preserved in great folio manuscripts of vellum, of which the earliest surviving were written in the twelfth century. There are three important twelfth century manuscripts, the Book of Noughaval, commonly called the Book of Leinster, in

Trinity College, the Book of the Dun Cow in the Royal Irish Academy, and a MS. the Irish title of which has been lost, listed as Rawlinson B 502, in the Bodleian Library at Oxford. Next in importance is the Yellow Book of Lecan, written towards the end of the 14th century and preserved in Trinity College. These are certainly copied from earlier manuscripts now lost, for the language of many of the sagas is as old as the ninth century, if we may judge from the very ancient language of some poems and law-tracts which survive.

The Mythological Cycle is the earliest in time, as it deals with heroes who were thought to have lived in Ireland before the coming of the Gaels. It is the chief source of knowledge of the religion of the pagan Irish. And very little is known about their religion. They believed in a happy Otherworld in the western sea where some of the gods dwell and which heroes sometimes were allowed to visit. It is not a heaven to which men go after death, but a happy island, *Tír na nÓg,* where there is no death or old age. Oisín went there with Niamh of the Golden Hair, and after three days he came back to Ireland to find that he had been away for three hundred years, and that all his companions were dead.

Besides this notion of an island (or islands) beyond the sea, there is a tradition that a race of supernatural beings inhabited Ireland before the coming of the Gaels, and that they withdrew into fairy-mounds all over the country where they still dwell, and whence they sometimes emerge to interfere in the affairs of men. These two traditions have become much confused, and we probably have to do with a blend of pre-Celtic and Celtic religious ideas. (It may be said in passing that there seem in Greece also to have been two mythologies, the gods of Homer, and others such as Demeter and Persephone, associated with agriculture, who play no part in heroic tradition.) A few of the names of these divine beings are good Celtic names, and evidently came in with the Celtic immigrants perhaps as early as 1500 B.C.

Chief of the gods is the Dagda ('Good God'). Oengus is his son, and Boann (the river Boyne) is the mother of Oengus. Lug is another, and his name occurs in the place-name *Lugdunum* in various parts of Europe where Celts have dwelt. The common name for all is Tuatha Dé Danann, peoples of the goddess Danu, of whom nothing further is known. There is a British Don, who is probably the same divinity.

Alfred Nutt suggested that the association of the gods with earth-mounds (such as New Grange, which was the dwelling of Oengus) went back to a stage of nature-worship when rivers, trees, wells and mounds were worshipped. He went on to suggest a common origin for certain features of Greek and Irish mythology, specially the doctrine of re-birth, which was part of the cult of Dionysus and which you will notice in the story I am going to tell. For Étaín is re-born three times, first by falling into the cup of a mortal queen while she is bewitched in the form of a fly, and again as the daughter of Eochaid Airem, king of Ireland, while her mother is in the fairy-mound of Brí Léith, and finally as the daughter of this third Étaín.

Before I come to the story of Étaín in the Mythological Cycle, let me tell you briefly about the other cycles of heroic tales or sagas. The Ulster Cycle is that of which Cú Chulainn is the central figure. King Conor Mac Nessa is king of Ulster and Maeve is queen of Connacht; the traditional date is the first century of the Christian era. These are the tales which Lady Gregory made into a book in her *Cuchullin of Muirthemne,* and which gave

Yeats many themes for his plays and poems. The longest saga, and one which is epic in scale and temper, is the famous Cattle-Raid of Cooley (*Táin Bó Cúailnge*), the story of Cú Chulainn's defense of Ulster, alone against the whole army of Queen Maeve. The noblest saga, and probably the finest in all Irish literature, is the story of Deirdre and the Sons of Uisneach. Then there is Bricriu's Feast, full of interest and humour, and the story of Mac Da Thó's Pig, in which champions contend for the hero's portion at a feast, as we are told the Gaulish warriors used to do in Caesar's time. These are the sagas we have chosen for discussion. There are many others that I would gladly have included.

The Fenian Cycle is later in time, being set in the reign of Cormac Mac Airt, who was supposed to have reigned at Tara in the third century. These are the tales of Fionn and Oisín and Caoilte, of Conán Maol and Goll Mac Morna, many of which may still be heard from story-tellers in the Gaeltacht. *The Pursuit of Diarmuit and Gráinne* is the Fenian love-story. And the last survivors of the Fenians are made to live on into St. Patrick's time, so that we have a famous tale called The Colloquy of the Ancients (*Acallam na Senórach*) which Professor Gerard Murphy will tell you about.

And last come the Cycles of the Kings, from which we have found room for only two stories, one of them having to do with the birth of King Cormac Mac Airt and his accession to the Kingship of Tara (there is a parallel here to the Roman legend of Romulus and Remus), the other a saga about a young queen married to an old husband and her love for her stepson. It is a motif which occurs in ancient Greek tradition, and which supplies the theme of T. C. Murray's *Autumn Fire*. There are some seventy sagas in this Historical Cycle, some of them about legendary kings, many about historical persons, and they are not without moments of pathos and of humour. Some of them were made into poetry by Ferguson a hundred years ago, when there was more interest in these traditions than there is now.

A.E. once said: 'We have often thought a book surpassing the *Arabian Nights* might be made by a writer of genius who would weld into a continuous narrative the tales of the Gods, the Fianna and the Red Branch, so full of beauty, mystery and magnificence that, as the raw material for romance, there is hardly anything to equal them in the legendary literature of other countries.'

The wooing of Étaín is one of the two chief tales of the Mythological Cycle. (The other is *The Battle of Moytura,* which you shall hear about next time). It is in the Book of the Dun Cow, but owing to loss of leaves a great deal of it was missing, and scholars had made various attempts to supply the lost passages. Then some twenty years ago Dr. Best made an exciting discovery. He was examining the Irish manuscripts in the Phillipps Collection at Cheltenham, when he saw among them a gathering of parchment leaves which looked familiar, and he recognised it as part of the famous Yellow Book of Lecan. And these leaves, which are now in the National Library, contain the complete text of the *Wooing of Étaín*. It has since been published in *Ériu xii.*

The chief points that have been cleared up by the discovery of the complete text concern details of the relationship between various mythological persons, and I shall not discuss them. But one matter is worth mention because it gave rise to more than one false scent, and serves to show how hazardous it is to guess the answer to a problem in mythology. At a certain point in the story, as you shall hear, Étaín was changed into a beautiful fly by the curse of a jealous wife, and in this form she was carried out to sea by the wind. Oengus rescued her and kept her in a glass cage which he carried about with him. He fed her with flowers. The passage describing her transformation is missing from the Book of the Dun Cow, which was the only manuscript known until Best discovered the lost leaves of the Yellow Book of Lecan. Zimmer, indeed, made a shrewd guess at what must have happened in the missing part of the story. But other scholars gave rein to their imaginations. Sir John Rhys in his *Arthurian Legend* decided that Oengus was the Celtic Zeus, and Étaín the goddess of Dawn. 'Her dwelling in the glass house which the god carried about with him seems to be a sort of picture of the expanse of the heavens lit up by the light of the sun.' Alfred Nutt thought rather of Snow White in her glass coffin watched by the seven dwarfs. Roger Loomis seized upon the diet of flowers, and sought to equate Étaín with Persephone of Greek mythology, who was gathering flowers when she was carried off to Hades. Étaín, he says, is a flower-maiden and moon-maiden. It is now plain that Étaín had been changed into a fly, and the glass cage and the flowers are no longer a problem.

Now to the story, which dates from the ninth century in its present form. There are indeed three stories, but they form a sequence and appear as a sequence in the two manuscripts which contain them. There is a strange beauty here which perhaps no other Irish story shares. The temper of love is there, and the power of magic, and a happy ending. It is one story in three, as it were, a comedy in three acts. The Dagda became the lover of Boann, wife of Elcmar of the Bruig (New Grange), and from their union was born Oengus. He was given in fosterage to Midir of Brí Léith (near Ardagh, Co. Longford). Later when Oengus had grown to be a man, and was in possession of the Bruig, Midir came to visit him. While he was there he suffered an injury and he claimed in compensation the fairest maiden in Ireland, Étaín the daughter of Ailill. Oengus won her from her father for Midir with the Dagda's help, by clearing twelve plains and making twelve rivers and giving her weight in gold and silver.

Midir returned home with the beautiful Étaín, but his first wife, Fuamnach, struck her with a magic quicken rod and turned her into a pool of water. The heat of the air and of the earth turned the water into a worm, and the worm became a purple fly of wonderful size and beauty. Its music was sweet, and the air was fragrant around it. The fly was always with Midir, and he knew that it was Étaín. Then Fuamnach drove her away by causing a magic wind which carried her out on to the rocks and waves of the sea. For seven years she was in misery until she alighted one day on the breast of Oengus himself. For some time he carried her about in a sun-lit cage of crystal, but the jealous Fuamnach got to know of it and drove her away again. This time she came to rest on the roof of a house in Ulster, and fell into the cup of one of the women in the house, the wife of Étar who was an Ulster king. The woman swallowed the fly, and she was re-born as the daughter of Étar. It was a thousand and twelve years from the time of her birth as daughter of the fairy Ailill to the time of her birth in the house of Étar.

That is the end of the first story.

The second story begins after the interval of a thousand years, when the Tuatha Dé Danann have retired into their fairy-mounds and the Gaels are established in Ireland. But we are still in a period of pure legend, so you must not expect any dates. The king of Ireland in this story was succeeded by a king whose son was killed in Da Derga's Hostel shortly before the period of Cú Chulainn and the Ulster heroes, according to the learned tradition.

When Eochaid Airem became king of Ireland, the people refused to pay tribute to a king who had no queen. He sent out messengers to find the loveliest girl in Ireland, and they brought him Étaín the daughter of Étar. Eochaid had a brother Ailill, and he fell sick for love of Étaín, and none could cure him. Eochaid went on his royal circuit of Ireland, leaving Étaín to care for Ailill, so that his grave might be dug, his lamentation made and his cattle slain. (The slaying of a dead man's cattle is of some interest for the religious ideas of the pagan Irish).

One day, as they were together in the house, Ailill confessed to Étaín the cause of his sickness, and she said that she would gladly cure him with her love, but that it might not be in the house of the king. She made a tryst with him on the hill about the court. But at the hour appointed, a magic sleep came upon Ailill, and a man in the likeness of Ailill came in his stead to keep the tryst with Étaín. Three times this happened, and the third time Étaín protested that it was not with him that she had made the tryst. The stranger said: 'It were fitter for you to come to me, for when you were Étaín daughter of Ailill, I was your husband.' And he told her that he was Midir of Brí Léith, and that they had been parted by the sorcery of Fuamnach. He asked her to come away with him, and she refused to go without the consent of her husband, the king of Ireland.

That is the end of the second story.

III

The third story is in a form familiar to those of you who have heard folk-tales recited, or who have read Padraic Colum's book, *The King of Ireland's Son*. A stranger visits the hero and offers to play a game of cards (here it is a game of chess). The hero wins three times, but the stranger wins the last game, and lays a penalty on the hero.

I shall read you the opening of this story, following pretty closely the translation of Bergin and Best.

'Another time on a lovely summer day, Eochaid Airem king of Tara arose and climbed the terrace of Tara to gaze over Mag Breg. It was radiant with flowers of every colour. As Eochaid looked around, he saw a strange warrior on the terrace before him. A purple tunic was about him, and his hair was golden yellow and reached to his shoulders. His eyes were bright blue. He had a spear in one hand and a shield in the other with a white boss and ornament of gold...

Eochaid said 'Welcome to the warrior whom we do not know.' 'It is for that we have come,' said the warrior (That is to say: 'I come as a friend, not as an enemy'). 'We know you not,' said Eochaid. 'But I know you,' said the warrior. (Many of you will be reminded of the common episode in the folk-tales about the king of Ireland's Son: *Aithníonn tusa mise 7 ní aith-*

23

nim-se thú). 'What has brought you?' said Eochaid.
'To play chess with you,' said he... 'The queen is asleep,'
said Eochaid, 'and it is in her house that the chess is.'
'I have here,' said Midir, 'a set of chess that is as good.'
That was true: a silver board and golden men, and each
corner of the board lit up by a precious stone, and the
bag for the chessmen was of plaited links of bronze.'

They play three games of chess and Eochaid wins
each time, and Midir gives him rich prizes. The fourth
time they play for a stake to be named by the winner.
Midir wins the game, and the stake he claims is a kiss
from Étaín. Eochaid was vexed at that, but he bade
Midir come a month from that day to receive his prize.

On the day appointed Eochaid had gathered his warriors around him and the doors were locked. But Midir
appeared in the banqueting-hall. 'What is promised is
due,' he said. He put his arms around Étaín and rose
with her into the air and through the roof of the house;
and they flew away in the form of two swans.

Eochaid and his men set out to recover Étaín and attacked Brí Léith, the fairy-mound which was Midir's
home. He appeared before them and promised to restore Étaín. The next morning fifty women appeared at
Tara all like Étaín in form and dress, and Eochaid was
in doubt which one to choose. The one he chose turned
out to be not Étaín herself, but her daughter and his
daughter too, another Étaín. She bore him a child, and
the child was put out to die, as it was a child of incest.
It was found by a herdsman and he and his wife reared
the girl, and she prospered, for she was the daughter of
a king and queen. Etarscéle became King of Ireland,
and one day his people saw the herdsman's child and
told him of her beauty. She was Étaín reborn, and Etarscéle made her his wife, so that she was the mother of

Conaire son of Etarscéle.

This brings us to the opening chapter of the *Destruction of Da Derga's Hostel,* a saga of the Ulster Cycle which you shall hear later on. I may conclude with the description of this young Étaín at the beginning of that story. I first learned of it from A.E. who told me of this wonderful description to illustrate what he called the incandescent imagination of Irish story-tellers:

'He saw a woman at the edge of a well, and she had a silver comb with gold ornament. She was washing in a silver basin in which were four birds of gold, and bright little gems of purple carbuncle on the chasing of the basin. She wore a purple cloak of good fleece, held with silver brooches chased with gold, and a smock of green silk with gold embroidery. There were wonderful ornaments of animal design in gold and silver on her breast and shoulders. The sun shone upon her, so that the men saw the gold gleaming in the sunshine against the green silk. There were two golden tresses on her head, plaited in four, with a ball at the end of every lock. The color of her hair was like the flower of the iris in summer or like pure gold after it had been polished. She was undoing her hair to wash it, so that her arms were out from beneath her dress. White as the snow of one night were her hands, and her lovely cheeks were soft and even, red as the mountain foxglove. Her eyebrows were as black as a beetle's back. Her teeth were like a shower of pearls. Her eyes were as blue as the hyacinth, her lips as red as Parthian leather. High, smooth, soft, and white were her shoulders, clear white her long fingers. Her hands were long. White as the foam of a wave was her side, long and slender, yielding, smooth, soft as wool. Her thighs were warm and smooth and white; her knees small and round and hard and bright. Her shins were short and bright and straight. Her heels were even and lovely. If a rule had been laid upon her feet it would hardly have shown any imperfections in them, unless it should crease the flesh or the skin. The blushing light of the moon was in her noble face, a lofty pride in her smooth brow. The radiance of love was in her eyes; the flush of pleasure on her cheeks, now red as a calf's blood and changing again to snowy whiteness. There was gentle dignity in her voice. Her step was firm and graceful. She had the walk of a queen. She was the fairest, loveliest, finest that men's eyes had seen of all the women of the world. They thought she was of the fairies. Of her it was said: "All are lovely till compared with Étaín. All are fair till compared with Étaín".'

CATH MAIGE TUIRED

By Brian Ó Cuív

Names such as Parthalón, Fir Bolg, Tuatha Dé Danann, Míl Espáine and Gaedel Glas are familiar to us from our schooldays. We generally remember them from the first chapters of our history books where we read of ancient traditions of various colonisations or invasions of Ireland in the pre-Christian era, the last of which was supposed to be that of *clanna Míled,* the children of Míl, from whom the most important families in Ireland in historic times claimed descent. These traditions, as you may know, are to be found in the compilation known as *Lebor Gabála Érenn,* 'The Book of the Conquest of Ireland', of which a number of versions has survived in manuscripts dating from the twelfth century onwards. Scholars have disagreed as to the date of composition of the *Lebor Gabála.* Rudolf Thurneysen supposed that it was composed about the time of Ruaidrí Ua Conchubair, the last High-king of Ireland, – that is about 1160. On the other hand A. G. Van Hamel considered it probably at least a hundred and fifty years older than that, and T. F. O'Rahilly believed that a version of it was in existence in the early part of the ninth century. However we need not concern ourselves with discussion on this point. But we may note that already some eight hundred years ago the *Lebor Gabála* version of early Irish history had achieved a great degree of popularity, and this was reinforced later when in the seventeenth century Geoffrey Keating used it as the basis for the first part of his History of Ireland, *Foras Feasa ar Éirinn*. In this way, long after the formal teaching of these traditions in the bardic schools had ceased, they were kept alive among the people by humble scribes and popular poets.

Now it is quite clear that the *Lebor Gabála* is a deliberate work of fiction. It purports to enumerate the successive invasions of Ireland since the Deluge, but its artificial character is obvious from the heterogeneous material used in its construction, including, as it does, Biblical and classical sources as well as native traditions. It may be that by the time the Irish literati, equipped with the Latin learning of the Christian missionaries, came to write down their people's history on the model of Eusebius's 'Chronicles', the genuine native tradition of Irish origins was lost, and that there remained only a vague idea that their ancestors had come to Ireland from abroad. Or it may well be, as O'Rahilly has suggested, that the true aim of those who composed the *Lebor Gabála* was to obscure the real traditions of the various ethnic groups which had peopled this island. For here, before the Norse incursions, we had a mixed population drawn from original Celtic and non-Celtic elements. The Celts included both Goidelic and Brythonic peoples who had come here at different times, but the superiority of the Goidelic or Gaelic people, whether it was originally in numbers or in weapons, had won for them the dominant position in the country, and in time their language replaced the languages of all other groups, whether Celtic or non-Celtic. When unity of language had been achieved, the historians and genealogists set about creating the myth of unity of origin. Hence the genealogical lists which are found in such abundance in Irish manuscripts; hence, also, the artificial history of *Lebor Gabála Érenn*. Let us recall briefly the main sequence of events as told there.

Five people are represented as taking Ireland before the Gaeil. First came Cessair, daughter of Bith, son of Noah, who with fifty maidens and three men arrived here forty days before the Flood. All this company perished except Fintan mac Bóchra, who is supposed to have survived the Deluge and lived for 5,500 years thereafter. He turns up frequently in other contexts, and from his attributes of old age and omniscience may be identified with the Celtic God of the Otherworld. There may be some connection between the tradition of a woman as the first colonist and the concept, common throughout Irish literature, of the sovereignty of Ireland as personified by a woman.

Next came Parthalón, a descendant of Japhet, together with four chieftains, three hundred years after the Flood. In his time we have the beginnings of organised life. Plains were cleared, cattle introduced, houses built, and even ale brewed. Moreover the first battle ever to be fought in Ireland took place, in which Parthalón defeated a certain Cichol Gricenchoss of the Fomóraig, who are described as being one-armed and one-legged men. Incidentally elsewhere the Fomóraig, together with the *lupracánaig,* are described as monsters begotten by Noah's son Ham as a result of the curse put on him by his father. As we shall see, they play an important role in the Battle of Mag Tuired. Parthalón and his five thousand followers were finally cut off by the plague, but again there was one survivor to tell the tale, this time called Tuan mac Sdairn or Tuan mac Cairill, a further instance of the euhemerisation of the Otherworld God.

Thirty years after Parthalón came Nemed, son of

29

Agnoman, of the Greeks of Scythia. Again we are told of successful battles against the Fomóraig until at last Nemed, like Parthalón, died of plague. After his death his progeny were oppressed by the Fomóraig who obliged them to pay a heavy tribute at Mag Cétne each year at Samain. Eventually the children of Nemed became desperate and they attacked the stronghold of the Fomorians at Tor Conaind. In the ensuing fight most of the Nemedians were killed and the remainder left Ireland for good. Some went to live in Britain, some to 'the northern islands of the world', and one of them made his way back to Greece where his descendants lived in servitude for many years.

From them came the next people to invade Ireland. They were known as the Fir Bolg, a name which is explained as being due to the fact that they were forced while in Greece to make arable land by covering rocks with earth which they carried in *builg* or bags, or alternatively that it was because they brought bags of clay from Ireland to Greece as a protection against venomous reptiles, or because they used these bags to make vessels in which to sail to Ireland. O'Rahilly has argued convincingly that the name Fir Bolg has replaced an earlier population name *Builg,* which he takes to be that of a Brythonic group of Celts whose continental kinsfolk are familiar to us under the name Belgae. It is interesting to note that as long ago as 1685 Roderick O'Flaherty, an Irish antiquarian, had concluded that the names were identical.

These descendants of Nemed, who are also called Fir Domnann and Gáilióin, had five leaders when they came to Ireland, and they divided the land fivefold between them. They held the country for thirty-seven years and established the kingship of Ireland which was held by nine of their kings, the last of whom was Eochaid mac Eirc. Eochaid's reign is described as a fortunate one. A code of laws was introduced, harvests were good, and there was no rainfall but only dew, – a sure indication that Ireland had normally a rainy climate in ancient times just as today. This beneficent rule was rudely interrupted by the arrival of the fifth group of invaders, the Tuatha Dé Danann, who, like the Fir Bolg, were descended from Nemed. They were the progeny of those Nemedians who, as you remember, had retired to the northern islands of the worlds – *indse tuaiscertacha an domain* – after the battle at Conand's Tower. There they had learned wizardry and heathen lore and devilish knowledge, so that they were expert in every art. May we not perhaps see in the present-day use of the word *tuaisceartach* with the meaning 'sinister', 'uncivilized', an echo of some such old traditions?

The coming of the Tuatha Dé was the prelude to the battles of Mag Tuired about which I must tell you. According to the Lebor Gabála tradition there were two battles, separated by twenty-seven years, the first between the Fir Bolg and the newly-arrived Tuatha Dé Danann, and the second between the Tuatha Dé, now successfully established as rulers of Ireland, and our old friends the Fomóraig who, as you will have noticed, were conspicuous by their absence in the time of the Fir Bolg, – a circumstance which has led some scholars to regard the Fomóraig and Fir Bolg as identical. We shall see later that the theory of two separate battles of Mag Tuired has been seriously questioned, but first let us see how they are fitted into the traditional scheme of history.

The oldest copy of the Lebor Gabála, that in the twelfth-century Book of Leinster, describes the coming of the Tuatha Dé Danann in this way: 'Thus did they come, in dark clouds. They landed on the mountains of Conmaicne Réin in Connachta and they cast a darkness upon the sun for three days and three nights. They demanded battle or kingship of the Fir Bolg. A battle was fought between them, namely the first battle of Mag Tuired, in which there fell one hundred thousand of the Fir Bolg. After that they (that is the Tuatha Dé) took the kingship of Ireland.'

Such is the brief account of the battle. Other versions of the Lebor Gabála, describing the outcome, say that the remnants of the Fir Bolg retired after their defeat to the islands around Ireland, – Ara, Íle, Reachrann, and Inse Gall – and according to Mac Liag, poet of Brian Bóraime, some of them built the forts of Dunangus and Dunconor in the Aran Islands.

Now quite apart from the Lebor Gabála there is an account of the contest between the Fir Bolg and the Tuatha Dé Danann. Unfortunately only late and fragmentary copies have come down to us, so that we are unable to determine how far it derives from an old story. It opens with a summary of the wanderings of the children of Nemed and a long account of the invasion of the Fir Bolg. Then it turns to the Tuatha Dé and describes their arrival which is revealed to Eochaid mac Eirc in a dream.

'I saw a great flock of black birds', said the king, 'coming to us from the depths of the ocean. They settled over all of us, and fought with the people of Ireland. They brought confusion on us, and destroyed us. One of us, I thought, struck the noblest of the birds a blow and cut off one of its wings.'

Meanwhile the Tuatha Dé had landed and burnt their ships. They proceeded eastwards to Bréfne and encamped there. Then the Fir Bolg sent one of their warriors named Sreng to spy on the invaders. When the latter saw him they sent Bres, son of Elatha, to parley with him. The warriors met and held conversation, for, having common ancestors, they spoke the same language. They inspected one another's weapons and were duly impressed by them. Then Bres demanded battle or half of Ireland. Sreng returned to his people and counselled them to make a division of Ireland with the Tuatha Dé, but the Fir Bolg refused to do this and accepted the challenge of battle. Yet they asked for a delay, 'for', as they said, 'we shall have to prepare our spears, to mend our mail, to shape our helmets, to sharpen our swords, and to make suitable attire'. Moreover it was agreed that the Tuatha Dé should provide the spears for both sides and the Fir Bolg the javelins. Both armies prepared healing wells for their wounded, and at last after six weeks of summer had gone, the battle began. The description of it is long-winded and rhetorical, a common fault in later Irish tales. The two armies suffered great casualties, and the Tuatha Dé Danann king, Nuada, had his right arm severed at the shoulder by a blow from Sreng, thus fulfilling Eochaid's prophetic vision.

At length Eochaid mac Eirc, overcome by thirst, left the battle-field to go in search of a drink. The wizards of the Tuatha Dé, perceiving this, hid from him all the streams and rivers of Ireland so that he came to the strand of Eothail. There he was attacked by three warriors of the Tuatha Dé, and they fought till all four were slain. By the way, the incident of the burning thirst is reminiscent of another tale, *Togail Bruidne Da Derga*, about which you will be hearing in a later broadcast. After Eochaid's death, Sreng, now leader of the Fir Bolg, made peace with the Tuatha Dé, leaving them all Ireland except Connacht which he chose for his own people.

Thus ends the story of the first battle of Mag Tuired. O'Rahilly sees in it a basis of historical fact which he ingeniously relates to the Lebor Gabála traditions. His theory is that the invasion of Nemed represents the arrival of the Brythonic *Builg* (or Belgae) between the sixth and the fourth centuries B.C. The so-called Fir Bolg invasion is in reality an invasion by another Brythonic group, composed of Laigin, Domnainn, and Gáilióin, in the third century B.C. These inflicted a number of defeats on the earlier inhabitants, among them being the defeat of the Builg or Fir Bolg of Connacht at Mag Tuired, identified as Moytirra, near Lough Arrow, in Co. Sligo.

What, then of the Tuatha Dé Danann invasion and the second battle of Mag Tuired? There can be very little doubt that their place is among the traditions of immortals rather than those of real men. In short, the Tuatha Dé are the pantheon of *clanna Míled,* the Goidelic Celts who were the latest comers to our shores, and the battle between them and the Fomóraig, who were also immortals, is on all fours with the battles between similar groups of divinities to be found in Indo-European myth. In an attempt to obscure the mythological nature of this battle – a natural reaction on the part of a Christianized people – our literary men attached it to the invasion traditions and in this form it has come down to us. The accounts of it in the Lebor Gabála are meagre, but if we may judge from the frequent references to it in the literature from the year 1200 on, it seems to have been the most popular tale of the so-called mythological cycle.

The oldest version we now have is in a sixteenth-century manuscript, but it clearly goes back to an Old Irish source. The tale opens with an account of the invasion of the Tuatha Dé and the loss of Nuada's arm. We are told that Dian Cécht, the Irish Aesculapius, assisted by Creidne, the craftsman, fashioned for him a silver arm having full power of movement. Hence his name Nuada Aircetlám, which, by the way, has a counterpart, Lludd Llawereint, in Welsh mythology. Owing to Nuada's temporary disability the kingship was given to Bres, son of Elatha, whose mother was of the Tuatha Dé, but whose father was a Fomorian. This paved the way for new Fomorian impositions so severe that there was no smoke rising from a roof in Ireland that was not under tribute to them. Tuatha Dé Danann champions were forced to do menial service for them, Ogma as a carrier of wood and An Dagda, the Good God, as a builder of earthworks. We are told, moreover, that the Tuatha Dé grumbled against Bres personally, 'for their knives were not greased by him, and however often they visited him their breaths did not smell of ale'. Things came to a head when Coirpre a poet of the Tuatha Dé, was treated inhospitably. He, like Aniér mac Con Glinne in a later age, replied by composing a satire on his host, Bres, the first satire ever to be made in Ireland, it is said. Thereupon the Tuatha Dé expelled Bres, who forthwith went to his Fomorian kinsmen for help to regain his throne. Among those who allied themselves with him were Innech, son of Dé Domnann, king of Fomóraig, and Balar, grandson of Nét, whose daughter Eithne was mother of the Tuatha Dé warrior Lug Lámfhata.

Meanwhile Nuada was restored to the kingship. Here follows a long account of the arrival at a Tuatha Dé

Danann feast at Tara of Lug, who presents himself as one skilled in all the arts – *An Samildánach* – an episode which, curiously enough, is retold in a fourteenth-century poem in praise of Maurice Fitzgerald, second earl of Desmond. The Tuatha Dé, having decided to give battle to the Fomóraig, chose Lug as their leader. This brings us to the central theme of the story which is the enmity between Lug and Balar, culminating in the slaying of Balar by his grandson. In the early version this contest does not get much prominence. The preparations for the battle and the early stages of the fight are recounted in detail. Nuada was slain by Balar, and then Lug and Balar faced one another.

'A destructive eye had Balar. It used to be opened only on a battle-field. Four men used to lift up the lid of the eye with a handle which was through the lid. If he looked upon a host with that eye, though they were many thousands in number, they could not resist even a few young warriors. Thus had it that magical power. His father's druids were brewing charms. He came and looked through the window, and the smoke of the cooking went about his eye so that the poison of the brew was in it ever after.

The lid is raised from Balar's eye. Then Lug cast a sling-stone at him which carried the eye through his head. And so it was his own army that looked on it. And it fell on the host of the Fomorians and thrice nine of them died beside it, so that the crowns of their heads came against Innech son of Dé Domnann, and a gush of blood burst from his lips.'

The remainder of the tale deals with the rout of the Fomorians who were beaten back to the sea. So many warriors fell on both sides that 'their number could not be told till the stars of heaven, the sands of the seas, the flakes of snow, the dewdrops on a lawn, the hailstones, the grass under the feet of herds, and the horses of Manannán Mac Lir in a seastorm be numbered.' But after all Bres, the cause of the battle, was spared by Lug, after promising to perform certain duties for the Tuatha Dé. The tale ends with a doleful prophecy of the end of the world by Badb, the wargoddess:

> 'Summer without flowers,
> kine without milk,
> women without modesty,
> men without valour;
> captives without a king,
> woods without mast,
> sea without produce.'

This story is, on the whole, loosely constructed, and is obviously a recasting of an earlier legend totally unconnected with the Lebor Gabála, namely the slaying of Balar by Lug. The significance of this contest in the sphere of mythology is too deep a subject to be entered into here, but I may mention that O'Rahilly has marshalled a great deal of evidence to prove that Balar is the Celtic Sun-god who in mythological tradition was overcome by a divine Hero, personified here by Lug.

As I have already said, this was a popular tale, and there were obviously several versions of it current in the centuries following the Norman invasion. These must have differed from each other at quite a number of points. For instance, there is a Modern Irish retelling, found in a seventeenth century manuscript, according to which the destruction of Balar's eye did not bring about his death, for after a while he recovered and took part in the fighting. When Lug challenged him, he fled from the battlefield, and his flight brought him across the country to Howth, back to Mag Tuired, and thence south to Mizen Head in Cork. There Lug and he fought it out, and Balar was slain. Before he died, he reminded Lug that he was Balar's grandson, and he asked him for one request, – that Lug should cut off Balar's head and place it upon his own 'so that my prosperity and great fortune, my dread power and my valour may be thine.' Instead of doing this, however, Lug wisely placed the head on the top of a pillar-stone, whereupon the stone split into four pieces.

That these incidents are not very late additions to the story is evident from the fact that they are found independently in earlier texts. Thus, the story of the flight occurs in Middle Irish *dindshenchas,* or lore of place names, and the connection with Mizen Head is reflected in the Irish name of that southern promontory, *Carn Balair* or *Carn Í Néid,* which reminds us of the old name Belerion applied to Land's End in Britain. Most striking of all is the incident of the destructive head which is found in such widely disparate sources as a twelfth-century poem in *Duanaire Finn* and modern folklore.

Incidentally the importance of folklore in the study of the Lug-Balar story may be judged from the fact that many aspects of it, such as the circumstances of Lug's birth and the reason for the enmity between him and his grandfather, have been preserved in oral traditions, although generally obscured in the written literature.

There remains the question of the literary connection between the two battles of Mag Tuired. As I have told you T. F. O'Rahilly argued that the story of the first battle is a fictionisation of an actual historical event which occurred near Lough Arrow, the defeat of the *Builg* or Fir Bolg by the Laigin in the third century B.C.

This, according to him, was the first and last battle of Mag Tuired. He believed that the second battle was a mythological one, and as such could have no real location in Ireland or anywhere else, but that the later adaptors of this tale fitted it to the 'locals' of Mag Tuired known to them from the account of the real battle. Two obvious weaknesses in his case are, firstly, that the extant versions of the mythological second battle are considerably older in language than those of the first battle, and secondly, that our earliest records which speak of only one battle of Mag Tuired, invariably refer to that between the Tuatha Dé Danann and the Fomorians.

One point more: listeners who know the district of Moytirra in Co. Sligo may remember that it contains a great number of megalithic monuments which probably gave rise to the name Mag Tuired, 'Plain of the Pillars'. These monuments date from about 2,000 B.C., so obviously there is no question of their being associated with either of the battles which I have been discussing. Nevertheless it is quite possible that an Irish storyteller may have deliberately chosen such an impressive site for a tale, which, after all, must have been composed for a noble audience.

III

ECHTRA FERGUSA MAIC LÉTI

By D. A. Binchy

Nowadays one would not normally turn to lawyers in quest of either saga or epic legend. True, a cynic may sometimes feel tempted to suggest that our modern lawyers have their own mythology, peopled by shadowy figures like the 'reasonable man', the tenant to the *praecipe*, John Doe and Richard Roe, and all the rest of them. Yet even so, it is hard to realize that the profession which the layman is inclined to describe by the compound adjective 'dry-as-dust' had its origin – of all places – on Parnassus, and that the first lawyers were poets and prophets.

In ancient Ireland the connexion between the poet and the lawyer was very intimate. Indeed, the earliest records of Irish law are in verse, generally rather poor verse it must be confessed, designed to aid the student's memory in the days before the schools had committed their traditional lore to writing. There is even what purports to be an account of how, in the reign of Conor Mac Nessa (a name which by this time must have become familiar to you), the poets were deprived of judicature because the ordinary people complained that their judgements were so obscurely worded that nobody could understand them, and how a new caste of jurists – or 'brehons' – was established to replace them. Like so many stories of this kind, the legend has a basis of fact: it is just the usual attempt to push back into remote antiquity, into the heroic age, a change which really occurred much later when law became a separate science, expounded and applied by professional jurists.

Yet the jurists, too, retained many of the traditions of the poetic order, the *filid,* from whom they had hived off. In consequence the Irish legal records abound in references to the ancient mythology of the race. And there was another reason why the law-schools had a special interest in some of the old sagas. Like their modern successors, the Irish lawyers were great sticklers for precedent. They were always anxious to have a 'leading case' on which to hang a particular rule or institution; only they searched for such cases, not in the Law Reports, but in the sagas of the heroic age. Hence the origin of well-known rules – and more particularly of innovations in the law, such as the recognition of legal capacity to women – is always traced back to the action of some famous mythological figure and thus invested with the sanction of hallowed antiquity. Later, when Christianity had been adopted, the lawyers found another treasure-house of 'leading cases' in the Bible, and strangely enough in the Old Testament rather than the New.

Let me begin by giving you an example of their use of the Bible, because it illustrates very well the curious technique by which the jurists adapted a story to their special purpose. There is a rule in native Irish, as well as in modern Anglo-Irish, law that inadequacy of consideration is not in general a ground for avoiding a contract – or to translate into the language of laymen, that no matter how foolish a bargain you have made, provided you have entered into it legally, knowingly, and freely, you must perform your side of it. Now what 'leading case' do you think the jurists found for this rule? None other than the story of the Fall of Man in

Genesis; but the story is given a characteristic and highly unorthodox twist. The whole sorry business is regarded as a 'contract' between Adam and the Serpent, under which the entire human race was bartered for one apple. And Adam, though of course he had been shamefully overreached by the other party, was held to his agreement, and thus, says the text, 'the whole world perished' – meaning probably that death was introduced into the world – 'in exchange for a single apple'.

Note incidentally that the parties to this contract are Adam and the Devil; Eve, who after all plays the leading role in Genesis, is completely ignored. And rightly so from the standpoint of an Irish lawyer. For in the older Irish law a wife could not contract independently of her husband. She could at most act as his agent; and only if he had authorized her to do so, or afterwards expressly or impliedly ratified the agreement (as in this case Adam was held to have done by his subsequent conduct), was it regarded as a valid contract, but a contract to which he rather than she was bound.

I'm afraid the jurists took somewhat similar liberties with the native sagas they pressed into service. One can never be quite sure that the stories they tell have not been doctored to fit into the legal framework they are designed to illustrate. Some of these sagas survive in non-legal sources also and can therefore be checked, but to-night I am going to deal with one whose preservation (at least in its earliest form) we owe exclusively to the jurists.

First of all, however, I should like to say something about the general characteristics of the sagas found in the law-books. Nearly all of them belong to the Ulidian or Ulster cycle, but the story usually turns on a quarrel between the Ulaid and the Féni, two of the three principal races which once, according to the story-teller, divided Ireland between them, the third being the Gáilióin or Gáilni, who however play no part in the events related. Thus the opening words of our story, in its eighth-century version, are as follows: 'There were three chief races in Ireland, the Féni, the Ulaid, and the Gáilni i.e. the Laigin'. Now those of you who have read the late Prof. O'Rahilly's great work *Early Irish History and Mythology* will note the coincidence between this tripartite racial division and the order of the Celtic invaders of Ireland which he claims to have established: first, the Érainn, whose most important representatives were the Ulaid in the North; next the Lagenian tribes, whom he would identify with the Gáilióin (or Gáilni); and finally the Goidels, or as they called themselves in their own language the Féni, who arrived last and came direct from the Continent, not – like the other tribes – by way of Britain. It is true that the so-called 'Brehon law' is the law of these latest conquerors; yet in most of the stories which profess to trace the origin of a particular rule or institution of this law, we find the two races – the Ulaid or Érainn of the North and the Féni – agreeing to the rule or jointly accepting the judgement of one of the famous mythological law-finders. What is the point of this? I suggest that the jurists were anxious to represent their laws as the laws of the whole people and not those of a conquering minority, just as later the genealogists, with a rather similar object in view, forged Goidelic pedigrees for the aristocracy of the earlier races.

The saga I am now about to summarize for you also deals with a conflict between the Ulaid and the Féni. In a list of sagas preserved in three manuscripts it is called The Adventure *(Echtra)* of Fergus mac Léti (pronounced like English 'lady'), and the protagonist in the drama is a mythological king of Ulster, Fergus son of Léte. I spell his father's name so in deference to all the scholars who have hitherto mentioned him, though I have an idea that the *e* was short and that we should really call our hero Fergus mac Leti (pronounced 'leddy'). In the other Ulidian sagas he is merely a name in the list of kings and this fact lead my revered teacher Rudolf Thurneysen in his epoch-making work *Die Irische Helden- und Königsage* to dismiss our story as a late invention of the law-schools, quite unjustifiably as we shall see later on. The real reason why so little is recorded of Fergus mac Léti is, as O'Rahilly has observed, that he is a double of the better-known Ulidian hero Fergus mac Roich, who incidentally also met his death in water, though whether O'Rahilly is right when he goes on to state that both of them 'represent the Otherworld God under different designations' is a question which I am not competent to discuss. At all events there is one thing we do know about Fergus mac Léti outside our present story: in other sources he is numbered among the successive owners of the Caladbolg, the famous sword of Celtic mythology, both Goidelic and Brythonic, which across the water eventually becomes Arthur's sword Caliburnus and ends up as the 'brand Excalibur' in Tennyson's *Idylls of the King*. In our story, too, the Caladbolg plays its part, though here it is simply called Fergus's sword.

The saga tells how, while Fergus ruled over the Ulaid, a civil war broke out among the Féni, i.e. the Midland Goidels with their chief centre at Tara. There were in reality only two competitors for the over-kingship of the Féni, though the earliest recension of our story rather confusingly makes them into three. One was the celebrated Conn Cétchathach, Conn of the Hundred Battles, the ancestor-deity of the Midland Goidels; the other was his 'uncle' – that is of course according to the fictitious 'pedigree' provided for these mythological heroes – Eochu Bélbuide, Eochu of the Yellow Lips. Conn was ultimately victorious, and though Eochu had put up a fierce fight and done much damage, he was eventually driven out, fled northwards and placed himself under the protection of the Ulidian king. After a number of years he returned, still under the protection of Fergus, to his own country seeking to make peace with his kindred. But on his way south he was held up and slain by Asal, son of his rival Conn, and by the four sons of Buide son of Ainmire, probably a subordinate king of some Goidelic tribe; the sixth assassin was Buide's maternal grandson, a boy whom his daughter Dorn had borne to an 'outlander' i.e. to a non-Goidelic father.

Now in Irish law one of the gravest offences you could commit against a king or powerful magnate was called *díguin,* the violation of his protection by slaying someone whose safety he had guaranteed. Small wonder, then, that Fergus, breathing fire and fury, came into the territory of the Féni at the head of a mighty host to avenge this insult. Conn and his followers were unable to stand up to him; instead, they sued for peace and agreed to give Fergus full compensation for the offence against his honour. At this point the lawyers take control of the story for a few lines and go into elaborate details of the fines paid, with which I shall not weary you except for two items which have relevance for the sequel : (1) Conn himself, in atonement for his son's part in the affair, ceded to Fergus, i.e. to the Ulaid, a tract of territory belonging to the Féni. (According to the earlier version of the story it was situated in Mag Muirthemne just north of the Boyne, according to a later version it was farther south, the land round the mouth of the Delvin river N.W. of Balbriggan). (2) The sixth assassin, the son of the 'outlander', should really have been surrendered to Fergus, as the Féni were not responsible for his misdeeds; but his mother the Goidelic princess Dorn gave herself up in his stead and went into Fergus's household as a slave. And so the King of the Ulaid, his honour satisfied, made peace and returned home.

One day shortly afterwards Fergus and his charioteer drove to the sea – we are not told to what point of the coast – and overcome by the heat of the day they both settled down to have a sleep. While they slept the king had some strange visitors. Water-sprites suddenly swarmed out of the sea, lifted Fergus – still sound asleep – out of his chariot, having first taken good care to separate him from his famous sword, and bore him towards the water. Now the name given to these sprites has a topical interest even to-day: *lúchoirp* or *lúchorpáin,* lit. 'small bodies', a word which having undergone metathesis of the consonants *c* and *p,* survives as the modern Anglo-Irish 'leprechaun'. This is the earliest appearance of the leprechaun in Irish literature, and it is noteworthy that here he is clearly a water-sprite. An explanation of the word given in a very old glossary suggests the same thing, so it may be that originally the leprechaun was an aquatic or at all events an amphibious creature – a piece of information which might be worth passing on to Mr. Walt Disney should he honour us with another visit.

To return to Fergus. As soon as his feet touched the water, he awoke to find the little men swarming all about him. He grabbed hold of three of them, one of whom was on each hand and one on his chest. The latter was apparently their leader or king; at all events it was he who appealed for quarter, using the traditional formula for which we may call unconditional surrender. And Fergus made the traditional reply: 'Yes, if you give me the three things I shall choose.' 'You shall have them,' said the dwarf, 'provided they are in our power.' As a matter of fact Fergus asked only for one thing: a charm which would enable him to go about under water like the leprechauns. This he was given, though the eighth-century redactor of the saga was unable to decide between conflicting accounts of the nature of the charm: according to some it consisted of what we would now call ear-plugs made from herbs; according to others the king of the little men gave him his tunic, and Fergus, when he had wound it round his head (perhaps like a modern diving-helmet), could travel under sea, river and lake at will.

But there was one restriction on the use of the charm. The leprechaun warned Fergus that he was never to try it in Loch Rudraige, the modern Dundrum Bay, Co. Down, which was of course in his own territory. Here we have an echo of some primitive tribal taboo. The name of the loch is the same as that of an eponymous ancestor of the Ulaid, who are often called Clann Rudraige, though whether the loch got its name from the ancestor or the ancestor was invented to account for the name of the loch is uncertain. I think the second is more likely, for Rudraige must originally have been the name not of a man but of a whole tribe.

I suppose you can guess the sequel. The lure of the forbidden was too strong for Fergus, so one day he bade his charioteer drive him to the shore of Dundrum Bay and plunged into the loch. While he was swimming under water he suddenly found himself confronted with a *muirdris*, a dreadful sea-monster, whose movements are vividly described by the story-teller: 'At one moment it would blow itself out and the next moment it would contract itself like a smith's bellows.' The mere sight of it filled Fergus with such terror that his mouth was wrenched backwards and he dashed out of the water with his face contorted in a permanent rictus. Although he could not see this disfigurement himself, he guessed that something had happened to him, for he asked his charioteer: 'What do I look like to you?' The charioteer, though doubtless horrified at the change in the King's appearance, was diplomatic enough to conceal his dismay. 'You look badly,' he said, 'but a sleep will set you up again.' Thereupon Fergus allowed himself to be bedded in his chariot and straightway fell into an exhausted sleep.

The charioteer on the other hand, while his master slept, drove back in haste to Emain Macha, near Armagh, the principal seat of the Ulidian monarchy, and told the assembled elders of the disaster that had befallen their King. This confronted them with a very grave problem. In ancient Ireland no person with a serious physical blemish could hold the kingship, and a reigning king who suffered such a blemish was compelled to abdicate. But it would seem that Fergus was beloved as well as famous, for the wise men at once entered into a conspiracy to keep him on the throne and to conceal his blemished condition from him – I suppose because if he learned of it, he would himself feel bound to abandon the kingship. Anyway they devised the following scheme: the royal house of Emain was to be completely cleared of all strangers and base-born folk who might betray the secret; the king was then to be brought back and served only by such retainers as could be trusted to keep him in ignorance of his disfigurement; and in particular his head was always to be washed while he was lying on his back, not in the usual posture of leaning forward lest he should see his reflection in the water. The chances of getting away with this deception would not seem very bright; yet the plan worked for seven years, and Fergus remained their King.

But there was one person still in his service whom the elders would have been wise to remove. This was Dorn, the princess of Féni, who had become his slave in order to save her son from his vengeance. And she, it seems, took her turn with the royal ablutions. One day he told her to wash his head. He thought she was very slow in making her preparations and at last, in a fit of exasperation, he struck her with a whip. We can imagine how a proud and high-born woman would react to such treatment; in the story-teller's words 'resentment overwhelmed her, and she taunted him to his face with his blemish'. I suppose Fergus took the time to throw one glance at his reflection in the water and see for himself that what she had said was only too true; the next moment he had drawn his famous sword and cut her in two.

He then turned and drove straight to Loch Rudraige to find and conquer the monster that had terrified him; doubtless he felt that as his disfigurement had been created by fear, it would be taken away if he could triumph over the object of his fear. At all events he plunged in once more, and for a whole day and night he battled under water with the monster. The Ulaid collected along the sea-shore and watched with tense anxiety the whole loch seething like a cauldron and the mighty waves breaking on the beach. In the end they saw their King emerge from the water and climb up on

Fertas Rudraige, the old name for the sandbank which still separates the inner from the outer bay of Dundrum. He brandished aloft the head of the monster and had only just strength to call out to them proudly; 'I am the survivor' – in other words 'I've won' – when he fell back dead into the water. He had conquered his fear, but at the cost of his life.

Not a bad story, as sagas go. But the question now arises: what interest had the jurists in preserving it? What rule of law was it supposed to explain? Well, you remember the tract of land which the Féni had ceded to Fergus as part of the compensation for the slaying of his protégé. By a complicated legal argument with which I shall not weary you the jurists sought to show that this conveyance lapsed with the slaying of Dorn and that the Féni were entitled to resume possession of their territory. For various reasons a great many years elapsed before representatives of the Féni did actually come north to make their claim for the land, and their method of claiming it was to seize and carry off some of the cattle that were grazing on it. This procedure was acquiesced in by the contemporary Ulidian king, and such was the first case of *athgabáil*, taking, of distress, which ever after remained the principal legal remedy among the Irish. Needless to say this addendum was tacked on by the jurists and has no connexion with the preceding saga, any more than the saga itself has any connexion with the evolution of distraint, a method of enforcing legal claims which is common to all primitive societies. But we can be thankful that the lawyers manipulated the end of the story for their own purposes, because had they not concocted a 'leading case' out of it, the saga would almost certainly have been lost.

It remains to say a word about dates. Thurneysen believed that the story was invented in the law-schools as late as the 11th century. But when he expressed this opinion he was unaware that there survived among the unpublished legal manuscripts a recension of the story which, on linguistic grounds alone, must be dated as early as the eighth century. A few years ago I edited this recension in *Ériu,* and in the interval an American Celtic scholar has taken me to task for not dating it earlier still; he would put it at the end of the seventh century. On the whole I feel inclined to stick to my own date, but at least both of us are agreed that the text is very early, certainly three centuries earlier than Thurneysen's estimate. In any event we can trace the existence of the saga back well behind this prose recension. An archaic poem at the beginning of the old law-tract on Distraint recites in obscure and cryptic language the main 'facts' of this leading case, so that the *story* must be at least as old as the seventh, perhaps even the sixth century. Hence, far from being a late 'invention' of the law-schools, as Thurneysen thought, the saga is an early and authentic member of the Ulidian cycle.

Finally, a word about its subsequent history. In the late Middle Ages some enterprising redactor got hold of the saga and blew it up into a very Rabelaisian fairy tale in which the king of the leprechauns plays a more prominent role than Fergus himself. This tale was edited and translated by Standish Hayes O'Grady in his *Silva Gadelica.* And about fifty years ago Canon Peter O'Leary – an t-Athair Peadar – produced a carefully bowdlerized version of it in the modern dialect of West Munster. Those of you who have read *Eisirt* in your school days may be surprised to learn that the rudiments of the story – *ceithre cnámha an sgéil* – go back at least twelve centuries, indeed were probably told in court and camp long before Irish became a written language. It only goes to show that old sagas, like old soldiers, never die.

IV

LONGAS MACC N-UISNIG

By E. G. Quin

'Nathos is on the deep, and Althos, that beam of youth.
Ardan is near his brothers. They move in the gloom of
their course. The sons of Usnoth move in darkness, from
the wrath of Cairbar of Erin. Who is that, dim by their
side? The night has covered her beauty. Her hair sighs
on ocean's winds. Her robe streams in dusky wreaths.
She is like the fair spirit of heaven in the midst of his
shadowy mist. Who is it but Darthula, the first of Erin's
maids?'

This is the kind of language in which the story of
Deirdre and the sons of Uisnech impinged for the first
time on the outside world and made its contribution to
the beginnings of the romantic movement in European
literature. The passage is from *Darthula: a poem,* by
James Macpherson, and I shall return to it later. But
my first duty is to follow it backwards instead of for-
wards, and to give you the earliest available information about Nathos, Althos and Ardan, about Cairbar,
and above all about Darthula. Originally they are
Noíse, Ainnle and Ardán, Conchubar (whom I shall call
Conor) and Deirdre, five characters from among the
many who appear in the collection of tales we call the
Ulster cycle of Irish saga.

The title of the oldest version of the story is *The exile
of the sons of Uisnech.* Conor king of Ulster and his
court are on a visit to the house of Fedlimid the story-
teller. Towards the end of the feast Fedlimid's wife is

53

discovered to be in childbirth. The child cries out in its mother's womb, and the men of Ulster are so terrified that they appeal to Conor's druid, who prophesies, in partly obscure verse, that the child will be a girl, that her name will be Deirdre, that she will be beautiful, and that she will be the cause of great slaughter of Ulstermen and devastation in Conor's kingdon. Deirdre is born, and the warriors quite naturally want to kill her at once. 'Nay,' says Conor, 'I shall take her and rear her and make her my wife.' And the men of Ulster dare not go against him. For as a character in Synge's play says: 'in the end of all there's none can go against Conor... for if any went against Conor it's sorrows he'd earn and the shortening of his day of life.'

Deirdre is brought up in a place apart, and no one is allowed near her except her foster-parents and, as the Irish says, 'Lebarcham, for no one could do anything about *her*, for she was a female satirist; and everything, good or evil, that was done in Ireland she used to relate to the king in the House of the Red Branch at the end of the day.' The girl grows up, and of course becomes the most beautiful young woman in Ireland. And one winter's day her fosterfather is skinning a calf in the snow. A raven stoops to drink the blood, and Deirdre says to Lebarcham: 'Dear would be the man who had those three colours – hair like the raven, a cheek like blood and a body like snow.' Lebarcham has the very man for her. He is Noíse, son of Uisnech, and he is near at hand with his brothers Ainnle and Ardán. A meeting is arranged – by Deirdre, and Noíse, by a mixture of wheedling and threats of everlasting shame and contempt, is induced to elope with her. So off the three brothers go with their retinue, and Deirdre.

Conor sees to it that they do not stay long in Ireland.

So they try Scotland, where they enter the service of the king of Scotland. Wisely, they conceal Deirdre, but eventually she is discovered, and their troubles begin again. The king sends his steward to woo her in secret for him. Deirdre listens respectfully, but tells it all to Noíse each evening. Next the sons of Uisnech are sent on dangerous missions, but they survive them all. Finally all the men of Scotland come together to eliminate these three thorns in their king's side. But Deirdre is in the plot. She informs Noíse, and she and the brothers make a timely escape.

Meanwhile the men of Ulster are concerned that the sons of Uisnech 'should be in danger of death in enemy country because of an evil woman'. Conor appears to relent, and the brothers are invited back to Ulster under the protection of three warriors, chief of whom is Fergus, who are to guarantee their safety. They come, and to make assurance doubly sure Noíse will not eat till he has eaten with Conor. For the feast is a sacred thing, and he hopes that Conor is really prepared to bury all unkindness. Fergus is prevented by a trick from escorting them all the way. He compromises by sending his son with the brothers to give them safe keeping. And so they come to Emania, Conor's capital. Conor has just concluded a peace with a long-standing enemy, Eogan son of Durthacht, and Eogan's part of the bargain is evidently to do Conor's dirty work for him. With Conor's mercenaries around him to protect him he goes to meet the sons of Uisnech, and here I can do no better than quote the Irish: 'Eogan welcomes them with a blow of a great spear at Noíse, so that it broke his back.' There is killing then on all sides, and Deirdre is brought to Conor. When Fergus and the other guarantors hear what has happened they come to Emania, and after more bloodshed Fergus departs to Connacht, there to join forces with Ailill and Medb, who are king and queen there. And in a later story we find him fighting, admittedly rather half-heartedly, against Ulster.

Deirdre is with Conor for a year, and during that time, the story says, 'she neither laughed, nor ate nor slept her fill, nor raised her head from her knee'. She gives vent to her grief in impressive verse –

> Though fair you deem the fierce warriors
> who pace across Emania,
> more proudly stepped towards their house
> the three valiant sons of Uisnech.

> Him I deemed fairest under the sun
> and those who were dearest
> you have taken from me, foul the deed,
> nor shall I see them again.

And Conor, finding he can do nothing with her, says: 'What is most hateful to you of all you see?' 'You,' she replies, 'and Eogan son of Durthacht.' 'Then you will spend a year with Eogan,' says Conor. And as the three of them drive towards Armagh he mocks her with a raw jest. She dashes her head against a rock and dies.

I should like to call your attention to one or two points of a purely literary nature in this remarkable story. Firstly, the quite theatrical beginning. Deirdre is about to be born. She is to be a *femme fatale* if ever there was one. Conor, one can guess, is an unscrupulous tyrant. All the elements of tragedy are present. The tragic happenings are in fact vaguely foretold, and the tale, as it is unfolded, is not really much more than a filling-in process. Not that there is anything very original in all this. It is the usual method in an Irish tragic story, where every step is made to seem fore-ordained. And indeed the omens and prognostications at Deirdre's birth are really of a kind with the sheeted dead squeaking and gibbering in the Roman streets.

Next, the incident of the three colours. Overdone as this kind of thing is in folk-tales and fairy-tales, it in some way retains its effectiveness, and specially in our story, where it may be considered as the trigger which releases the whole action.

And finally Deirdre herself, at once the heroine and the villain of the piece. To begin with she is masterful, scheming and dangerous. But at the end of the story, when all schemings are forgotten, she is a tragic figure of a stature to do credit to a Shakespeare or a Racine.

The Irish text of this story occurs in three manuscripts, the oldest and best known of which is the 12th-century Book of Leinster. But this version of the tale is much older than the manuscripts in which it is preserved. The language of the prose sections in fact points to the 8th or 9th century as the date of composition, and some of the verse is undoubtedly older, possibly by a century or two. Behind this again we have presumably a period of floating traditions, and then, of course, the mists of antiquity.

For modern scholarship will not allow any historical authenticity to this or the other Ulster stories. To hold that Conor, Deirdre and the sons of Uisnech ever existed as human beings is to stand revealed as a euhemerist, one who mistakenly maintains that purely mythical characters were historical personages. Anyway stories about a princess who goes off with three brothers are known in other literatures. And the fact that such a story occurs in Sanscrit seems to indicate that we must look outside Ireland, though not necessarily in India, for its beginnings.

Four editions of this version have been published. First we have, from as long ago as 1808, an edition by Theophilus O'Flanagan. The title-page is worth quoting: 'Deirdre, or the lamentable fate of the sons of Usnach, an ancient dramatic Irish tale, one of the three tragic stories of Erin; literally translated into English, from an original Gaelic manuscript, with notes and observations: to which is annexed the old historic facts on which the story is founded.'

Next, in 1862, Eugene O'Curry published the text from the Yellow Book of Lecan, a later manuscript than the Book of Leinster. But the edition most of us have used till quite recently has been that by the German scholar Ernst Windisch in his *Irische Texte* of 1880; and this is the first edition that conforms to modern standards of scholarship. For nearly seventy years Windisch's edition held the field. Now we have a new one, a copiously-annotated edition published by the American scholar Professor Vernam Hull in 1949.

To turn from the asperities of the old-Irish version to the polished prose of the 17th-century Geoffrey Keating is like port after stormy seas. In his beautiful, classical language he tells us the same story, precisely, elegantly, his early modern Irish here and there echoing most effectively the phraseology of the original. I think Keating's must be the most perfect telling there is of the story, a masterpiece of economical statement where nothing is lost. Everyone who knows modern

Irish should read it.

But long before Keating's time an expanded form of the story had taken shape. Quite a number of the old stories have these later versions, some in middle Irish, some, like this one, in early modern Irish. They are usually long and detailed. They go in for series of alliterating adjectives and are full of purple passages. To a modern taste this is not nearly so attractive as the simple, terse style of the old versions. But the *Death of the sons of Uisnech* is an exception. It is perhaps a bit on the long side in one place, and the poems it contains are, with one or two exceptions, rather undistinguished. But the prose style is, for a late text, simple and felicitous. Further, it contains some details which help us with the older version and which may be survivals of really old tradition. It has a new title: *The tragic death of the sons of Uisnech.* Rather curiously, all the introductory matter about the birth of Deirdre, her wooing of Noíse, and the flight to Scotland is taken as read. The story begins with the men of Ulster deciding that the sons of Uisnech, the three torches of valour of the Gael, should be brought back from Scotland. Conor knows that Noíse will come back only if his safety is guaranteed by one of three warriors – Cú Chulainn, Conall Cernach, or Fergus. He interviews each of these in turn to find out what their reactions would be, if he, Conor, tried any tricks while Noíse was under their protection. Conall and Cú Chulainn make no bones about it. They would have the blood of many Irishmen, but Conor's above all. Fergus, however, is a little vague, and Conor, seeing a loophole, sends him to fetch the sons of Uisnech. He has some difficulty in inducing them to come, for Deirdre sees through the whole thing. She has dreamt, she says, that three birds came from

Emania with three drops of honey in their beaks, left
the honey behind and went away with three drops of
blood. The honey is Fergus's message, for honey is no
sweeter than a message of peace, and the three drops
of blood are the three sons of Uisnech. But her dreams
and her arguments do no good, and the journey back to
Ireland begins. And here Deirdre recites her beautiful
poem:

> Dear the land, that land in the east,
> Alba with its wonders,
> never would I leave it
> but that I must go with Noíse.

And so they arrive in Ireland. Conor is ready for them.
His minion, Borrach, in order to prevent Fergus from
going straight on to Emania, invites him to a feast, and
Fergus may not refuse such an invitation. He asks Noíse
what he ought to do. But it is Deirdre who replies:
'Abandon the sons of Uisnech if you must, yet to abandon them is a high price for a feast.' Fergus does his
best. He sends his two sons with them to Emania, and
his own word. Deirdre is still full of doubts, and has
some more disagreeable dreams. She wants them to go
to Dundalk to Cú Chulainn, but this, they reply, would
be an insult to Fergus's two sons. They arrive at Emania
·and are quartered in the House of the Red Branch, not
in Conor's own house, and this they take to be a bad
sign. Conor sends Lebarcham 'to see if Deirdre still
retains her form and beauty, for if she does,' he says,
'there is not of the race of Adam a woman fairer than
she.' Lebarcham, however, is on the side of the angels,
and tries to make Conor believe that Deirdre has lost
her looks. But he eventually gets at the truth, and the

fight begins. No impression at all is made on the sons of Uisnech. And in the end Conor perforce calls on his druid, who renders them powerless by his magic arts. 'Let me be killed first,' says Ardán, 'for I am the youngest.' 'Not so,' says Ainnle, 'but let me be killed first.' 'Nay,' says Noíse, 'I have a sword which Manannán mac Lir gave me, and it leaves no trace behind it. Let it be wielded on all three of us together so that no one of us may see the beheading of his brother.' And so it is done.

The rest of the story is as before, except that Cú Chulainn takes part in the avenging of the three brothers, and Deirdre's death is differently described. Before she dies, she laments the dead heroes:

> Long is the day without the sons of Uisnech,
> not wearisome was it to be with them,
> royal princes generous to the stranger,
> three lions from Cnoc na hUama.

> The three dragons of Dún Monaidh,
> the three warriors from the Red Branch,
> short will be my life after them,
> those three victorious in every onset.

The earliest manuscript containing this version of our story belongs to the end of the fifteenth century, and is preserved in the National Library of Scotland. The best edition is that published by the great Whitley Stokes in 1887. Stokes was a particular friend of Windisch's and his edition of the Death of the Sons of Uisnech appears in the second volume of the *Irische Texte* I have already mentioned.

During the modern Irish period our story becomes

associated with two others of a similar type, the 'Death of the children of Lir' and the 'Death of the children of Tuireann'. The three tales together come to be known as the 'Three sorrows of story-telling', the 'Three tragic tales of Erin', as O'Flanagan called them, and it is in this setting that most students of Irish come to know the story. The version used is the one I have just related to you, with the beginning supplied from Keating. Rather oddly, it is not till this late period that Deirdre's name appears in the title.

In 1899 Douglas Hyde published the early portion only of a text which he found in a Belfast manuscript written at the turn of the 18th century. This deals in great detail with Deirdre's upbringing. It does not contain much value for students of the older versions, but it has some literary merit and it has since been edited in full. Folklore versions have been written down both in Ireland and Scotland, and our story seems to have had just as strong an oral tradition as the Ossianic stories, the stories about Finn and the Fianna, which is saying a good deal for its popularity.

Not the least remarkable thing about the Deirdre-story is the fascination it has had at all times for translators and adapters.

First of all there is James Macpherson, a Scot, who in the second half of the 18th century published a number of epics, as he called them, purporting to be translations of a third-century poet called Ossian. I must resist the temptation to talk at length about Macpherson. But as his *Darthula: a poem,* is based on the story of the sons of Uisnech perhaps I may be permitted to give him a few minutes. As briefly as possible then. Macpherson published his epics. The question of their authenticity immediately arose, he was asked to produce his originals; he never in fact did so in a satisfactory manner. And the great Macpherson controversy began. The scholars and men of letters took sides. Samuel Johnson made the famous statement that there was no such thing as a Gaelic manuscript above a hundred years old, Macpherson threatened violence, and Johnson decided to carry a heavy stick. Commissions were appointed, books were written; and a Macpherson bibliography would now fill a volume on its own. The truth is briefly this. Macpherson's epics, in that they claimed to be translations from a third-century poet, were forgeries. They were not even honest translations of the late materials actually used. Macpherson had travelled extensively in Scotland, where Gaelic (originally Irish) stories abounded in oral tradition and in late manuscripts. He assimilated as much as he could, and composed (it is the only possible word), composed his epics. Only here and there did he actually translate. The prose poem 'Darthula', from which my opening quotation was taken, will do as an example of his method. The poem itself, in so far as any story is concerned, is practically unintelligible, but it is preceded by an 'argument' giving the story in straightforward language. It is the story I have just told you, but changed and distorted so as to make Argyllshire the centre instead of Ulster, and with much admittedly clever alteration of proper names. As regards style, Macpherson seems to have been practically uninfluenced by anything in Irish or Scottish Gaelic. Possibly the strongest influence on him was that of the Authorised Version, and the more bearable passages remind one strongly of the poetical parts of the Bible. But he frequently deserted this excellent model. And Johnson's verdict cannot be denied: 'Sir, a man might write such stuff for ever if he would abandon his mind to it.'

Macpherson's works are now only for the lover of literary curiosities. Yet we must not forget that his 'Ossian' had a profound influence on European literature. Even for our own studies he has his importance. For by his very impostures he focussed attention on Gaelic manuscripts, and so ensured the continued existence of many which might otherwise have been destroyed. He is a baffling, intriguing, exasperating figure, exasperating because we cannot completely dismiss him.

I have a feeling of anti-climax in turning from the fascinating, unreadable Macpherson to present-day translations. But nowadays we like our sagas straight, and in the case of the story of the sons of Uisnech there are plenty of translations to choose from. There is that of Arthur Herbert Leahy, who in his *Heroic romances of Ireland*, published in 1905, translates the older version, with both metrical and literal translations of the verse. There is also a translation by Eleanor Hull in her *Cuchulain saga* (1898). And more recent ones are those by the Americans Cross and Slover, and that by Myles Dillon. In addition there are French and German translations, and even a Russian one.

We now come to more consciously literary efforts. Sir Samuel Ferguson, in his *Hibernian nights entertainments*, runs the two versions together very effectively. He translates the verse into English rhyming stanzas. You have already heard the following in a literal translation:

Fairwell to fair Alba, high house in the sun,

Fairwell to the mountain, the cliff and the dun.
Dun Sweeny, adieu, for my love cannot stay
And tarry I may not when love cries away.

Ferguson also wrote a one-act play on the theme in which the characters remain in view all the time and the scenery changes gradually from Scotland to Ulster. It is rather Shakespearian in blank verse.

Lady Gregory's *Cuchulain of Muirthemne* appeared in 1902, and is an omnibus of the Ulster stories. Her *Fate of the Children of Usnach* is a very readable conflation of the two versions, together with some other matter from more recent sources. I can recommend it. With Lady Gregory we come to the Anglo-Irish revival, and criticism of the works of this period is rather beyond my scope. All I want to do here is examine briefly the form in which the old story has survived in the work of the principal writers.

Before I say something about the plays I must mention James Stephens' *Deirdre* (1923). It is difficult to know what to call this book. Perhaps novel is the best word. I like specially the picture of Deirdre as a mischievous young tom-boy at the beginning, and the wonderful liveliness of Noíse's two brothers Ainnle and Ardán. Stephens has adhered to the old story (he seems to have followed Lady Gregory), but he has certainly clothed its ancient bones with plenty of flesh, not to say muscle.

Synge' *Deirdre of the Sorrows* opens with a visit to Deirdre by Conor. The first act consists of this and the elopement. The second is mainly devoted to the argument between Deirdre and Noíse as to whether they should leave Scotland or not. Synge makes Noíse hang back, while Deirdre fatalistically insists on returning to

Ireland. In the last act we have the return and the murder, with again something unexpected, Conor's humble wooing of Deirdre after he has killed the three brothers. Of all the *Deirdre's* I have looked at in English Synge's is easily the most effective. Many of you will have seen it on the Abbey stage, but it repays reading too for the splendour of the language and for its warmth and humanness.

Yeats' one-act play *Deirdre* is in blank verse. Again many of you will have seen it played. It deals only with the arrival back at Emania and the murder.

The third modern play is that by George Russell (Æ). In action it is close to Synge's play, but is without its unexpected twists. It is more frankly literary and lyrical and I find it completely charming.

I have now told you, I hope, about all the important forms of the Deirdre-story. For the Deirdre-story it is and always has been, in spite of the old titles. And here I should like to put a question, though I cannot answer it. We have the Deirdre-story in late old Irish, early modern Irish, contemporary Irish, Scottish Gaelic, and in various forms of English. If it is to survive, what form must it take in order that it may continue to say something to us? The answer depends on many things. While we wait for it, those of us who read Irish will go to the graceful, evocative Keating. All of us should read Synge, whose Levarcham may indeed have been right when she said that Deirdre would have a story that would be told for ever.

V

FLED BRICRENN

By M. A. O'Brien

Ten miles north of Newry, on the main Dublin-Belfast
road is the little village of Loughbrickland. Close to it,
in a wonderful setting of low hills and trees, is the small
lake of the same name. The older form was Loch Bri-
crenn, 'Bricriu's Lake', and it takes us back over the
span of nearly two thouand years to the hero or rather
the villain of our tale, 'The Feast of Bricriu'.

Bricriu was one of the Ultonian lords and lived at Dún
Rudraige, the present Dundrum, in the East of Ulster,
and his constant epithet, *biltenga* or *neimthenga* 'evil
or poison-tongue', aptly illustrates his character which
is well developed in our story. In a poem in our second
oldest all-Irish manuscript (Rawlinson B 502) this
quality of his is well described: 'On his face would rise
a blister as big as a fist, if he knew some secret concerning an honourable man and could not blab it at once'
and his own motto was 'Clearer to me is a whisper than
a cry to anyone else'.

To this evil trait of character he owed his death. The
young bull calf of the Brown Bull of Cooley and the
famous Connacht bull 'Whitehorn' meet on the plain of
Cruachain and fight for a whole day and night. Finally
the young bull is defeated and bellows. Fergus, the
exiled Ulster hero, and Ailill, king of Connacht, are
playing chess. 'What did the bull bellow?' said Maeve
to her herd. 'I know,' said Bricriu, 'the very strain you

67

sang in the morning.' Fergus glanced at him and struck with his fist at Bricriu, and the five chessmen in Fergus' hand went into his head, and it was for him a permanent hurt. Thus perished one of the Ulster lords.

The earliest version of our tale is found in our oldest Irish manuscript, The Book of the Dun Cow, written at Clonmacnoise about 1100. The origin of the name is curious. St. Ciarán, the founder of Clonmacnoise, has a favourite dun cow. On its death its skin was preserved as a holy relic of the saint in the monastery. A late story of the finding of the lost Táin, tells how Fergus, who had, of course, been dead several centuries, was brought to life and related the whole story to Ciarán, who wrote it down on the skin of his beloved cow. Now, our manuscript does contain the Táin, and was actually written at Clonmacnoise, so that it was quite natural for simple folk to believe that it had been made from the hide of Ciarán's dun cow.

The Book of the Dun Cow was published in facsimile by the Royal Irish Academy in 1871. It was, however, not a facsimile of the actual MS. but a reproduction of a copy made by the famous scribe Joseph O'Longan. It, of course, reproduced O'Longan's hand and for forty-two years misled Irish scholars in the belief that the original manuscript had all been written by one scribe. Only in 1912 did the great Irish palaeographer Dr. R. I. Best show that it was actually written by three different scribes.

Two of these working in turn produced the original manuscript before the year 1100, as one of them – Maelmuire – we know was murdered in 1106 by marauders. The third scribe – whose name is unknown, but whom we call the Interpolator – was at work perhaps two hundred years later. He had altered the original text considerably by adding passages from other versions of inferior value. But Dr. Best's discovery enables us to restore the original tale which, to judge by the language, was first committed to writing in the eighth century. The chronology then may be summed up as follows: date of composition unknown, but I shall later on venture to suggest that a primitive form of the story already existed even before the Celts came to Ireland; date of writing down: sometime in the eighth century; date of the oldest copy we have: about 1100; date of the interpolations: about 1250-1300.

There are three other and later manuscripts of the whole tale, but in all four the end is either missing or illegible. It is therefore particularly fortunate that the final section, perhaps the best told one, has been preserved separately in a manuscript now in Edinburgh.

But now to the tale itself.

True to his character Bricriu has plotted to set the three greatest Ulster heroes at variance. These were, Cú Chulainn, Loegaire the Triumphant, and Conall Cernach 'the Victorious'. To achieve his purpose he builds and furnishes a magnificent hall, a full description of which is given, and prepares a wonderful feast. To each of the three great heroes in turn he promises the 'Hero's Portion'. To Loegaire, for instance, he says: 'Sooth, if the champion's portion of my house be thine, the championship of Ulster is thine for ever. The champion's portion of my house is worth contesting, for it is not the portion of a fool's house. To it belongs a cauldron full of pure wine with room enough for three of the braves of Ulster: further a seven-year-old boar; since it was a piglet nothing has gone into its mouth but fresh-milk porridge and meal in the Spring, pure cream and milk in the Summer, kernels of nuts and pure wheat in the Autumn and meat and broth in Winter. There is a fattened cow seven years old; since it was a young calf nought has entered its mouth but fresh milk, meadow hay, and corn. Add to this five score wheaten cakes baked in honey. Such is the hero's portion of my house. And as you are the best hero among the Ultonians, it is but just to give it to you, and that is my own wish. When then, at nightfall, the feast is laid out, let your charioteer rise up and to him will be given the hero's portion.' 'There will be dead men,' said Loegaire, 'if it is not done so.' Bricriu laughed and his spirits rose.

In this way he succeeded in inciting the three great warriors to fight one another until they had to be pacified by Conor, the king of Ulster.

But not content with setting the men at variance, he plots in his mind how he can get their wives to quarrel also. Just when he has finished thinking, he sees Fedelm, wife of Loegaire, coming out from the palace with fifty women, rather hilarious after the banquet. He addresses her in flattering terms and promises her precedence over all the Ulster ladies if she but enter the hall first. In similar terms he addresses Lendabair, wife of Conall Cernach. Finally Emer, wife of Cú Chulainn emerges. 'Greetings, Emer,' said Bricriu 'wife of the best warrior in Ulster. Emer of the Fair Hair is a proper name for you. All Erin's kings and princes contend for you in jealous rivalry. As the sun surpasses the stars of Heaven, you outshine the women of the whole world, in form and shape and birth, in youth and beauty and fame, in reputation and wisdom and speech.'

The three bands of women then went out till they met together three ridges away from the hall, and none of the three was aware that Bricriu had incited the others. They proceeded to the hall. Even and graceful and steady was their progress on the first ridge, scarcely did each woman move one foot in front of the other, shorter and quicker were their steps on the second ridge, but on the third ridge each one vied with the others and each one raised her smock to be first to get into the hall – for what Bricriu had told each one, unknown to the others, was that she who should first enter the hall would be queen of the whole province.

No solution of the question of precedence was found in Emain, and Conor advises the three warriors to go to Cú Roí son of Dáire in the extreme south of Ireland for adjudication.

Loegaire then had his chariot yoked and he sprang into it and drove away. A dark, heavy dense mist overtook him so that he could drive no further on the path. 'Let us stay here,' said he to his charioteer, 'until this mist clears away.' Therewith he dismounts and his gillie puts the horses to graze in a neighbouring field. While the gillie is there he sees a vast spectre coming towards him. Not beautiful was his description: he was hard-headed, fat-lipped, with bulging eyes and bristly face, hideous, horrible and strong, stubborn, violent and haughty, fat and puffing, with enormous muscles and strong forearm, bold and audacious and uncouth. On his head short clipped hair, about him a dun-coloured mantle with a smock reaching to the ball of his rump. On his feet old tattered brogues, and over his back was hanging a ponderous club big as the wheel-shaft of a mill.

'Whose horses are these, lad?' said the giant, gazing furiously at him. 'Loegaire the Triumphant,' said the lad. 'True,' said the giant, 'good is the man whose steeds these are.' As he spoke, he raised his club and smote the

gillie from tip to toe. The lad called and Loegaire came
up. 'Why are you at him?' 'For ruining my pasture,'
said the giant. 'I shall be responsible,' said Loegaire.
They struggle together and Loegaire has to turn tail
and flee to Emain Macha, leaving his steeds and his
gillie and his arms.

Not long after this Conall Cernach came the same
way and reached the spot where the magic mist had
appeared to Loegaire. The same black, dark gloomy
cloud enveloped Conall so that he could not distinguish
earth or sky. He leaped from his chariot and his gillie
unyoked the horses in the same meadow. He was not
long there till he saw the same spectre coming towards
him. He asked him whose servant he was. 'I am the
servant of Conall the Victorious,' said the lad. 'He's a
good man,' said the giant, giving the lad a blow from
his ear to his ankle. The lad yelled and Conall came up.
The two fought but the giant got the better, and Conall
fled just like Loegaire, leaving his armour, his charioteer and his horses behind, and so came to Emain.

Cú Chulainn then came by the same way and reached
the very same spot and the same dark fog enveloped
him too. He sprang down from his chariot and Laeg
brought the horses into the meadow. He had not been
long there when he saw the same man coming towards
him, and he enquired whose gillie he was. 'I am Cú Chulainn's gillie,' said he. 'He's a fine fellow,' said the
giant, plying him with the club. Laeg yelled and Cú Chulainn came up, and he and the giant began wrestling
and pounding one another. Finally the giant was van-
quished and forced to give up the captured charioteers,
horses and arms. Then Cú Chulainn arrived back in
Emain Macha with his great booty and gave it back to
its rightful owners. 'Thine is the Warrior's Portion,'

said Bricriu to Cú Chulainn. 'It is clear from your deeds that you two have no right whatever to compete with him.' 'That shall not be true, Bricriu,' said the other two. 'For we know it was one of his fairy friends who came to us and inflicted shame on us and practised magic on us in the matter of the 'Champion's Portion,' and because of that we will not yield it to Cú Chulainn.'

As it was impossible to settle the matter, the Ulster nobles decided to go with the three heroes to Cruachain, the capital of Connacht, where lived Ailill and Maeve, and let the king of that province decide.

The whole host – king and warriors – set out for Cruachain, and here comes what is definitely the highlight of the whole story, the description of the Ulster hosts approaching the Connacht capital.

'With the speed and impetuosity which the Ulster warriors approached Cruachain a great trembling seized the palace so that the war-arms fell from the walls to the ground and fear seized the hosts of the fort so that every one in the royal palace stood trembling like a rush in a flowing stream. Maeve said: 'Since I came as queen to Cruachain I have never till today heard thunder with a cloudless sky.' Findabair daughter of the king and queen went to the sun-bower over the entrance to the fort and spoke: 'I see a charioteer coming into the plain, dear mother.' 'Describe him,' said Maeve, 'his shape, his form and his appearance, the colour of the horses and the course of the chariot.' Findabair then in exalted language describes the approach first of Loegaire the Triumphant, then Conall the Victorious and finally of Cú Chulainn, and it is only fair to say that here we have the finest descriptions in the Irish language. The style is highly rhetorical and exalted, and bristles with difficulties for the translator, but I cannot refrain from giving you Henderson's vigorous rendering of the passage describing the onrushing of Cú Chulainn, which, though slightly inaccurate in places, reproduces the spirit of the original:

'In the chariot a sad, melancholy man, comeliest of the men of Erin. Around him a soft crimson pleasing tunic, fastened across the breast, where it stands open, with a brooch of inlaid gold, against which his bosom heaves, beating in full strokes. A long-sleeved linen kirtle with a white hood, embroidered red with flaming gold is about him. Set in each of his eyes eight red dragon gem-stones. His two cheeks blue-white and blood-red. He emits sparks of fire and hissing breath with a ray of love in his look. A shower of pearls, methinks, has fallen into his mouth. Each of his eyebrows as black as the side of a black spit. On his two thighs rests a golden-hilted sword, and fastened to the copper frame of the chariot is a blood-red spear with a sharp mettle-some blade on a shaft of wood well fitted to his hand. Over both his shoulders a crimson shield with a rim of silver, chased with figures of animals in gold. He leaps the hero's salmon-leap into the air and does many like swift feats besides. Before him in the chariot there is a charioteer, a very slender, tall, much-freckled man. On his head very curly bright-red hair, with a fillet of bronze upon his brow which prevents the hair from falling over his face. On both sides of his head cups of gold confine the hair. About him a mantle with sleeves opening at the two elbows, and in his hand a goad of red gold with which he guides the horses.'

At Cruachain the prize is again awarded to Cú Chulainn, but Loegaire and Conall will not agree.

The last, and in many ways, the best-told section, of

the story is that entitled 'The Champion's Covenant'. In it is made the final decision as to the Hero's Portion. It occurs separately in the Edinburgh manuscript and commences, unlike all other sections, with the traditional 'story-opening' "Once upon a time". It may, therefore, at one time have been an independent tale, though the great German scholar Thurneysen did not think so. It opens with the Ulster warriors gathered in Emain, fatigued after their sport and games. 'As they were there, at eventide, they saw a huge, ugly churl coming towards them into the house. It seemed to them that there was not a single Ulster warrior who might reach his height. Ugly and horrible was his guise. Next his skin he wore an old hide and about him a dark dun-coloured mantle. Eyes yellow and ravenous protruded from his head, each one as big as a cauldron fit to take an ox. Each finger as stout as another man's wrist. In his left hand a block – a fit load for twenty yoke of oxen. In his right hand an axe, to the making of which had gone thrice fifty molten charges, with a handle which would take a team of six horses to carry it, and with an edge which would cut a hair aloft in the wind.'

He announces to the assembled warriors that he is seeking in Ulster something he could not find in the whole world, 'fair play'.

He proposes to cut off a warrior's head and come and have his own cut off next night. His proposal is treated with derision and he agrees to reverse the conditions of the contest, namely, to have his own head cut off by a warrior the first night and then to come back on the following night and cut that hero's head off. Three of the greatest Ulster warriors – Fatneck son of Shorthead, Loegaire the Triumphant and Conall Cernach agree to the proposed conditions. Each cuts off the churl's head, but each plays the coward and evades an encounter with the churl on the following night.

The fourth night the churl returned, and fierce and furious was his appearance. All the ladies of Ulster had come that night to behold the strange wonder that had come to the Red Branch. That night Cú Chulainn was also present. Then the churl began to upbraid them: 'Ye men of Ulster, your prowess and valour have come to an end. Greatly do your warriors covet the Champion's Portion, but they are unable to contest it. Where is that miserable wight you call Cú Chulainn? I want to know if his word is better than that of the other warriors.' 'I do not desire any bargain with you,' said Cú Chulainn. 'Yes indeed, I deem it likely you greatly fear death.'

Thereupon Cú Chulainn leaped towards him and dealt him a blow with his axe and hurled his head to the top rafter of the Red Branch, till the whole house rattled. Then he again caught up the head, gave it a blow with the handle and made smithereens of it. Then the churl rose up.

The following day the Ulstermen were watching Cú Chulainn to see if he also would evade the churl as the other warriors had done. When, however, they saw that Cú Chulainn was waiting for him, they became greatly dejected and deemed it proper to keen him, as they thought his life would only last till the churl arrived. Then said Cú Chulainn to Conor, 'By my shield and by my sword, I shall not go till I fulfil my pledge to the churl, for though death awaits me, I prefer death to dishonour.'

As they were there at close of day, they saw the churl approaching. 'Where is Cú Chulainn' said he. 'I am here,' said Cú Chulainn. 'Humble is your speech, you wretch,' said the churl, 'you greatly fear death. Yet though you fear, you do not try to avoid what you have bargained for.' Cú Chulainn came up and stretched his neck on the block. So big was the block that his neck but reached halfway across. 'Stretch out your neck, you wretch,' said the churl. 'You torture me,' said Cú Chulainn: 'Dispatch me quickly. I did not torment you last night.' 'I can't slay you,' said the churl, 'what with the size of the block and the shortness of your neck.'

Then Cú Chulainn stretched out his neck, so that a full-grown man's fist might fit between each two of his ribs, and his neck reached over to the other side of the block. The churl raised his axe till it reached the ridge-pole of the hall. The creaking of the old hide the churl wore and the rattle of the axe being raised aloft with all the strength of his two hands were as the loud noise of a wood tempest-tossed in a night of storm.

Down it came on his neck – with the blunt side below, while the Ulster warriors stared in amazement. 'Rise up, Cú Chulainn; vain it is for any warrior from Ulster or Ireland to think of competing with you in bravery, valour or truth. Yours is the sovranty of the warriors of Ireland henceforth, and the 'Hero's Portion' unchallenged, and for your wife precedence of the women of Ulster into the banqueting-hall, and I swear by the oath of my people that whosoever shall challenge your right from now on shall die immediately.' From that on Cú Chulainn's right to the 'Hero's Portion' was never challenged.

From this short outline of the story you will see that it is, in the main, based on two separate motives: (a) The Contest for the 'Hero's Portion', and, in the last chapter (b) 'The Champion's Bargain', the agreement to allow oneself to be killed.

Here we have two very precious survivals linking the Celts of Ireland with those of Western Europe. We know about them only from the statements of classical writers, and one of these, Posidonius the Stoic, who lived in the last century B.C. – just over two thousand years ago, and who had travelled extensively in Western Europe, is quoted as the authority for the following:

'There was a custom at Celtic feasts in ancient times, that when the joints were set before the guests the bravest man would take the thigh. If anyone else laid claim to it, then the two rose up to fight till one of them was slain. And other men in the gathering, having received some silver or gold coins, or even a certain number of jars of wine, having taken pledges that the gifts promised would really be given and having distributed them among their friends and relations, would lie down on boards, face upwards, and allow some bystander to cut their throats with a sword.'

Here we distinctly see the two motives of our story; first the Contest for the 'Hero's Portion', and secondly – in a slightly mutilated form – 'The Champion's Bargain'. Posidonius relates this as having been the practice 'in ancient times', but perhaps what he really heard was something like a primitive Celtic version of 'The Feast of Bricriu'.

VI

SCÉLA MUICCE MEICC DA THÓ

By Nora K. Chadwick

The lectures which you have been listening to in this course will have made it clear to you that Ireland has a richer heritage of saga literature than any other country in the world. The number of prose stories preserved in early manuscripts is enormous, to say nothing of numerous variant versions. The range and variety of subjects is even more astonishing, as the examples in the present course also show. The heroic sagas, which relate to the prowess of the heroes of the far past, are perhaps, the most numerous, and this gives us a clue as to which were the choice favourites of the Irish professional story-tellers and their audience. This is the class of sagas to which the story of *Mac Da Thó's Pig* belongs.

The love of the Irish of the Ancient World for heroic and historical sagas is clearly stated in the latest of them, which relates to the Battle of Allen fought in 722 between the High-King of all Ireland and the provincial king of Leinster. We are told here that the High-King's army agreed to march if a certain Donn Bó went with them – 'For Donn Bó was the best teller of king-stories in the world.' He refused to recite on the first occasion when called upon, however, and his place was taken by Hua Maiglinni, who is described as *ríg-drúth Érenn,* and who is said to have begun reciting the battles and valiant deeds of the Northern Half of Ireland and of Leinster from the *Destruction of Dinn*

Ríg down to his own time. In other words, his repertoire was comprehensive, and the excellence of his professional manner of recital was without equal.

This high standard of memory and of art must have done much to keep alive the history, and the historical conditions of the Heroic Age. It gives form and body to the laconic notes attached to the royal names in the genealogical poems of Munster and Leinster, but especially of Leinster – poems which have been preserved from the seventh, and even from the sixth centuries. Indeed the nucleus of the ancient traditions has been so well preserved that we are in danger of forgetting that the attitude of the saga-teller to his subject, and his artistic methods, gradually changed. At times his own political views colour his presentation of the facts. We shall see that the views of the author of our saga are against Ulster and favour Connacht. The Ulster story-tellers had their great prose epic the *Táin Bó Cuailnge*, 'The Cattle-raid of Cuailnge', so the story-tellers of the other provinces felt that they must try to do as well for their own people. But indeed by the time the *Story of Mac Da Thó's Pig* was composed, the story-teller does not take even the political issues very seriously. What he liked was a good tale, and he knew how to tell one.

The *Scéla Muicce Meicc Da Thó*, 'Tidings of Mac Da Thó's Pig', as our earliest version calls it, is one of the most brilliantly told of the early Irish sagas, and it purports to give a picture of the old heroic life in Ireland and its warlike spirit. It is a very early story, probably composed in its present form about 800 A.D. The scene of the story, and its familiarity with Kildare, suggest that the author belonged to Leinster, and inherited its fine heroic tradition. But the *Story of Mac Da Thó's*

Pig is a more sophisticated production than the *Battle of Allen*. It belongs to the early period of the Viking regime, and this may have done something to substitute laconic humour and a spirit of ripe burlesque for the dignity and poetical beauty which makes the story of Donn Bó and the *Battle of Allen* to me the most exquisite treasure of the Irish sagas.

The *Story of Mac Thó's Pig* has been preserved in at least six manuscripts. The Book of Leinster, written about 1160, is the earliest. The best form of the story is preserved in this version, and in H.3.18 (in the paper leaves) now in Trinity College, Dublin; and in Harley 5280, written in the first half of the sixteenth century and now in the British Museum. But these three texts are independent of one another. They seem to be derived from a common source, which was itself a transcript of a previous version, believed from its language to date from about 800. A fourth version, Rawlinson B. 512, was written in the fifteenth century and is preserved in the Bodleian Library at Oxford. This is less accurate and less conservative than the first three. There are two further manuscripts, one in the National Library of Scotland [Ms. XXXVI] and another [H.6.8.] in Trinity College, Dublin. These represent a modernisation of the story, perhaps made in the sixteenth century. So it is clear that the story has been a favourite from the earliest times, almost to the time of our great-grand-fathers; and even in our own day the late Professor Tomás Ó Máille of Galway has retold the story in a delightful modern version.

The theme of the story, the central point on which the narrative turns, is the '*Champion's Portion*', the right of the greatest champion at a feast to receive the *curadmír*, the 'Hero's Portion', from a great central cauldron containing the communal supply. Naturally where a great body of heroes are gathered together this distinction never passes unchallenged, and a claimant must make good his right, first of all by producing his own credentials, boasting his own deeds of valour; and secondly by quashing the objections and counter-claims made by his opponents and rivals. If he does not succeed in making good his claim the matter may be taken to arbitration, and this, as we have seen, is what happened at Bricriu's Feast. Indeed something like a burlesque of arbitration occurs at the close of our own story, where it is claimed that the men of Connacht receive too small a share, and Mac Da Thó looses his dog on them all in the hope that its sagacity will lead it to bite the right party; but this is anticipating our story.

What I want to emphasise here, before proceeding to tell the tale, is the antiquity of its theme. It is probably the most anciently attested of all Celtic stories. Among the ancient Celtic peoples, just as in heroic society elsewhere even today, the most important of all social functions is the communal feast, which is always an occasion of high ceremony. Accounts of these heroic feasts among the ancient Celtic peoples of the Continent have been left us by many ancient writers, notably Athenaeus (IV 40), who derived his information from Posidonius; and these accounts of Gaulish feasts are so similar to thoses of ancient Ireland that some of them could be transferred into an Irish saga without causing the least surprise.

Listen, for example, to Diodorus Siculus, writing of the Gauls: 'When they dine... they have hearths with big fires and cauldrons and spits loaded with big joints of meat. They honour distinguished men with the best portions of the meat... And when they are dining some of the company often fall into an altercation and challenge one another to single combat – they make nothing of death. Whenever anyone will accept their challenges they set about glorifying the valour of their forefathers and boasting of their own prowess; and at the same time they deride and belittle their opponent, and try by their speeches to rob him of all the courage he has in his heart.' So also in our Irish saga of *Mac Da Thó's Pig*. We see the feast, with the heroes seated round great cauldrons, the bravest of them in the middle of the circle. We see the 'Champion's Portion' consisting of a whole hind quarter of pork, and the rivalry, among the heroes for such 'honour portions'. Here too we hear of the fantastic value set on bravery, which also found its echo in *Bricriu's Feast*.

In the *Story of Mac Da Thó's Pig* the contest for the Champion's Portion lies between the royal provinces of Connacht and of Ulster, and resolves itself finally into the rivalry of two heroes, Cet Mac Mágach of Connacht and Conall Cernach of Ulster. We are among the personnel of the great prose epic, the *Táin Bó Cuailnge*, but with the notable difference that Cú Chulainn is never mentioned. Since the saga makes mention of some thirty heroes the omission can not be accidental. It is probably an indication of the antiquity of the tradition of our story, before the development of the *Cú Chulainn Cycle*. However that may be, our laughing story-teller turns both these great rival dynasties to ridicule by the cunning of Mac Da Thó, king of Leinster. And again we are tempted to conjecture that our story is inspired by the claim of Leinster to supersede both Ulster and Connacht. It is significant that Mac Da Thó claims to derive his wisdom from the legendary High-King, Crimthann Nía Náir, who was believed to be reigning when

Christ was born, according to the Irish annalists, and who lies buried on the Hill of Howth. Crimthann possessed many famous treasures besides his wisdom, among them a pair of greyhounds. One wonders, if Mac Da Thó's famous hound laid claim to this pedigree.

Mac Da Thó, so the story goes, was a famous king of Leinster, who possessed a hound Ailbe. Ailbe defended the whole province and was renowned throughout Ireland. Ailill and Maeve, king and queen of Connacht, sent messengers to Mac Da Thó, demanding the dog; but at the same time messengers arrived from Conchobar, king of Ulster, making the same demand. Mac Da Thó was in a dilemma. Sleep and appetite deserted him. At this point we have a poem in dialogue between himself and his wife. She has observed her husband's restlessness and loss of interest in his food and asks what ails him. At first he refuses to tell her and brusquely declares that Crimthann Nía Náir has said you should never tell your secrets to a woman; but he gives way under pressure, and his wife hits on the really brilliant solution: he must promise the dog to both parties, and let them fight it out themselves.

Now comes an inimitable passage of compressed humour. Mac Da Thó takes the messengers from Connacht aside privately, and gravely announces that after much anxious perplexity he has decided to give the hound to Ailill and Maeve, and he bids them come to receive it formally. He then takes aside the messengers from Ulster, and makes the same promise to Conchobar, with the same condition. Both parties are secretly trysted by him for the same day, and both duly arrive simultaneously at the door of Mac Da Thó's hall. Mendaciously Mac Da Thó expresses his surprise –

'We did not expect you; but come along in, all of you,'

and he assigns them seats on opposite sides of the hall. We are not surprised to be told that the faces were not those of friends at a feast which were in that house. Mac Da Thó, with masterly indifference to the electric atmosphere, acts as his own steward, blandly welcoming his guests to a superb pig which he has slaughtered for them. It is Bricriu, the usual instigator of strife, who suggests that the pig be divided in proportion to the respective deeds of valour of the heroes present.

'Let it be done,' says Ailill, king of Connacht.

'Very proper,' says Conchobar, but then he ignites the straw by reminding Ailill that there are heroes present among his Ulstermen who have raided the Borders between the two kingdoms of Ulster and Connacht.

At first the challenge is taken up by the heroes of West Munster, who are on the side of Connacht. Before long one of their number, Cet Mac Mágach, makes good his claim to supremacy and takes knife in hand and sits down beside the pig. At this point he offers combat to any hero who shall gainsay his right to divide. Each after each the heroes of Ulster stand up to deny his supremacy, but ever and anon Cet shames them to silence by a well-aimed gibe at some defeat and humiliation in the past of every one of them, and the whole wordy contest takes up the greater part of the saga. We are thus presented dramatically with a rather unusual catalogue of the engagements in which the heroes of Ulster have been defeated in the past.

'And in this manner,' says the story, 'Cet flouted the whole province.'

But just as he is flourishing his knife with intent to divide the pig, who should bound into the house but the great Ulster champion, Conall Cernach. The men of Ulster give a roar of welcome; but Conall remarks coolly:

'I am glad that my portion is ready for me. Who is he who is doing the dividing out for you?'

An obscure dialogue in the most archaic form of Irish poetry called *retoric* now takes place between Conall and Cet, and at the end Cet reluctantly acknowledges Conall the greater hero, regretfully adding that if a certain Ánluan had been present he would have challenged Conall. –

'He is present though,' cries Conall, who at this point takes the head of Ánluan which is hanging at his belt, and flings it at his opponent. We here remind ourselves that head-hunting was a prevalent practice among the ancient Gauls. This is the climax of the feast. There is no further challenge, and Conall goes to make division of the pig, himself devouring the hind quarters – 'a load for nine men' – and a champion's portion indeed! He gives to the men of Connacht only the fore-quarters.

Now the men of Connacht resent the smallness of their portion and a turmoil arises. Mac Da Thó, sees his chance, and looses the hound Ailbe at the combatants, trusting to it to make its own choice as to which party it will attack. Both parties burst out of the house and away, and the hound gives chase and sets to slaughtering the men of Connacht, but Fer Loga, the royal charioteer of Connacht, rides it down with his chariot, splitting its head on the chariot pole. Here we get a touch of antiquarianism dear to the ancient Irish, for we are told that *Mag nAilbe,* 'Ailbe's Plain', the valley of the River Barrow, takes its name from this incident.

Both the parties of Connacht and of Ulster are now in full flight, and their course is traced northwards through Kildare and Rathangan and westwards through Meath. At this point the Connacht charioteer Fer Loga hides in the heather, and as Conchobar's chariot approaches he springs up behind him and seizes him round the throat.

'Buy your freedom, now, Conchobar,' he cries.

'Make your own terms,' replies Conchobar. – What else could he say?

'This it is,' says Fer Loga, 'the young women of Ulster must sing every night for a year: "Fer Loga is my darling." '

Thus it was, and at the end of the year Conchobar was fain to send him back to Connacht loaded with presents. The sympathies of the story-teller remain hostile to Ulster to the end.

The tale is told with brilliant narrative power. Terse and humorous, with laconic brevity, it reminds us of the Icelandic sagas at their best. The dialogue in particular is masterly in its understatement and crisp repartee. And in the few remarks made by Mac Da Thó to his visitors, all his previous train of thought, all his cunning and address, are suggested in a few brief words intended by him to hide his true designs from his guests, while suggesting to ourselves his hidden intention. Throughout the story not a word is wasted, no statement is expanded. The utmost condensation and economy have produced a little gem of a tale.

Yet with all its literary finish the story is essentially a tale to be told. The movement is swift. There is a total absence of reflection. The narrative aims at arousing and riveting attention and exciting interest, not at stimulating thought. The story-teller makes use of the element of surprise, of quick developments and dramatic moments. He seeks to impress by rapid crescendo to a startling climax, and a shock, when Cet reluctantly gives precedence to Conall Cernach in the absence of Ánluan.

'If Ánluan were in the house he would offer you yet another contest. It is a pity for us that he is not in the house.'

'He is though,' said Conall, taking the head of Ánluan from his belt, and hurling it at the breast of his opponent with such violence that a gush of blood burst through Cet's lips.

The warlike spirit and crude customs of heroic society are vividly brought before us in this lively little tale. It is essentially a story for men. The heroic details of Cet's previous encounters with the Ulster heroes are calculated to appeal to men rather than to women. Women indeed play very little part. We are in the atmosphere of an ancient heroic club-room. What a contrast to the refined and delicately handled story of Eochaid and Étaín and their supernatural adventures with the god Midir of the síd-mound Brí Léith; or to the poetical beauty of the story of Deirdre and the sons of Uisneach; or even to the later Cycle of stories of Finn and his heroes – stories of life in the open – of hunting, and romance, and of the magie and prowess of a simpler and less organised society than that of Mac Da Thó's feast! The gulf that separates these stories from our own and from one another is some measure of the range of theme which the early Irish story-tellers had at their command.

But the picture given us in the *Story of Mac Da Thó's Pig* is not a wholly savage one. There is more than a touch of humorous hyperbole in Conall's throwing the head of Ánluan at Cet. The feast is conducted according to strict rules. A recognised etiquette is observed; certain rules of precedence and fair play are the order of the day. The fact that these regulations and conventions are portrayed in their break-down does not alter the fact of their implication. *The Story of Mac Da Thó's Pig* is a glorious travesty of the Ancient World by one who honoured and laughed at its traditions.

The composer of our story must have been an intellectual with a wide range of literary knowledge. Within the small compass of this brief little tale he introduces many literary conventions well known from other sagas. Besides the themes of the 'Champion's Portion', the boasting and challenging at feasts, the stupendous appetite of the hero, there are a number of conventions of literary technique. We have seen that place-name speculation has its part to play, and the geographical details of Ailbe's route, as the hound gives chase to the royal guests, recalls the course taken by the boar Twrch Trwyth in the Welsh eleventh century story of *Kuhlwch and Olwen,* and in Irish *Dinnshenchas* stories. The reference to the ancient High-King Crimthann Nía Náir as a sage is particularly interesting. Then there is the dialogue poem between Cet and Conall in archaic retorics, and a dialogue poem between Mac Da Thó and his wife in the later strophic form of rhyme and assonance. The retorics are doubtless older than the saga; and the story-teller was evidently well acquainted with all matter relative to his story, as well as with all fashions and conventions current in early Irish literature.

The story itself seems to have been well-known in literary circles. Even before the period of our earliest manuscript text in the Book of Leinster (LL fo. 151a), an *Orgain Mic Da Thó* is included in the list of *prím-scéla,* 'primary stories', or 'chief stories' which the *filid* or professional poets of ancient Ireland used to relate to kings and chiefs. The list itself is probably of

89

tenth century date; but the tale is mentioned in a poem by Flannacán Mac Cellaich who is said to have been slain by the Norsemen in 896. The hostel of Mac Da Thó is one of a number cited in a poem on the halls or 'hostels', *bruidne,* of ancient Ireland.

The story was evidently much liked in later times also, for it forms the subject of a number of independent poems. None of these seem to be based directly on the text of our saga, and indeed I suspect they are inspired by a different version of the story. For instance, in two of the poems the real hero is not the dog Ailbe but the pig; and this is probably an original feature, for it is implied in the title of the story – *The Story of Mac Da Thó's Pig.* One of the poems is practically a panegyric on the pig. A pig is a strange hero for a story, even a grand big fellow like the one which supplies Mac Da Thó's feast. But we remember the great boar Twrch Trwyth in the Welsh medieval story of *Kulhwch and Olwen,* which gave so much trouble to King Arthur and his men; and in the Irish *Glossary of Cormac,* King of Cashel († 908) Twrch Trwyth is said to be in reality a prince.

The poetical versions of our story have quite a lot of additional matter to tell us too. The name of Mac Da Thó's wife is given, and those of his two sons, and of his grandson Léna who originally found the pig in Slieve Bloom and was responsible for its nourishment till it had seven inches of fat on its snout. A poor return it was the pig made him by grubbing up earth with its snout and burying him alive in his sleep. Mac Da Thó's wife, Maine Athrai, needed the pig for her husband's great feast. Léna had refused it, but on his death Mac Da Thó's swineherd Follscaide duly delivered the pig to his master. We can see from this how much our saga has omitted, and how much was known from elsewhere.

There can be no doubt that the entire story has been subject to wide variation. Its close analogy to *Bricriu's Feast* is universally recognised, yet not easy to explain. In *Bricriu's Feast* the story again turns on the 'Champion's Portion' and the dispute as to the hero who has a right to it. But there the decision is taken to arbitration, and a sophisticated element is introduced by the dispute and unseemly struggle for precedence carried on between the wives of the heroes. There also the ultimate decision in favour of Cú Chulainn as champion suggests a later version than that of our story. What is its relationship to our saga? Can oral tradition transform variant versions of an identical theme into two stories differing as widely as these?

One thing we can say with confidence. Our prose saga of Mac Da Thó's Pig is a work of art of high quality in its own right. Without a touch of romance, without the glamour of magic or of the supernatural, almost without antiquarian elements, it holds us throughout by its swift unflagging narrative, the rapid pitch and toss of its dialogue, the brilliant quality of the dramatic presentation. Never has the tradition of the Irish Heroic Age received a more compelling form – so much so that an earlier generation of scholars looked upon it as a direct and truthful presentation of the warlike spirit of its time. Yet Irish court life was never really like this; nor are we much nearer the truth in calling it a parody. Perhaps we may say rather that a literary genius has presented us with a well-preserved heroic tradition, seen through the prismatic lens of a later age. He brings to his theme a ripe sophistication, a concentrated irony, and a gay and lighthearted hyperbole. He puts criticism out of court and compels the hearer to his own mood by the sheer force of his high-spirited and unerring narrative gift.

VII

TÁIN BÓ CÚAILNGE

By David Greene

People who deal with early Irish literature usually refer to *Táin Bó Cúailnge* simply as 'the Táin'. This is
partly a handy abbreviation, but it is also the usage
in Irish literature and it tells us something about the
story; it is the original Táin, and the other stories whose
titles begin with *Táin Bó* are all either later stories or
old ones which have been re-worked to bring them into
relationship with the Táin as *remscéla* – preliminary
stories. And to use the simple word Táin for the original
saga helps us to glide over a small difficulty. We always translate *Táin Bó Cúailnge* as 'the cattle-raid of
Cooley', but why don't we say *Táin Bó gCúailnge* in
Irish? Of course eclipsis was seldom written in the Old
Irish period but the tradition of pronunciation was preserved, and I would expect eclipsis after a genitive
plural in later manuscripts, but I don't remember any
examples of *Táin Bó gCúailnge*. Not that the Táin
doesn't describe a cattle-raid – what in later Irish is
called a *creach* and in English a reiving – it certainly
does; Cú Chulainn's father, calling the Ulstermen to
battle, uses the stirring phrase 'men are being killed,
women are being captured, and cattle are being driven',
and Cú Chulainn is offered the release of the noble-
women and the dry cattle, or, alternatively, the slave-
women and the milch cows, if he will give up his snip-
ing at the Connacht forces. Two of the *remscéla* realise
the difficulty and refer to the forthcoming foray as *Táin*

inna mbó a Cuailngiu 'the driving of the cows from Cooley'. But, after all, this plundering of cattle and women was incidental to the main object of the expedition, that Connacht should gain possession of the great bull of Cooley, called variously *an Donn Cúailnge* and *an Dubh Cúailnge;* the name Donn is also that of the Old Irish god of the dead. Now, the word *bó* in Irish means only 'cow', but the corresponding word in other Indo-European languages – Sanskrit, for instance – can mean either 'bull' or 'cow', and I suggest to you that it's just possible that the title of our story originally meant 'The Driving of the Bull of Cooley'.

And why was this black bull of Cooley so badly wanted? Well, one of the versions of the Táin – not the oldest – gives us a nice rational interpretation. Ailill, king of Connacht, and his wife Maeve, chatting in bed one night, begin to argue about what each of them brought into the marriage. The argument grows so heated that they decide to compare their property on the spot, and, for every treasure that Ailill can produce, Maeve can find one to match it – except for one, a fine bull called Finnbheannach – Whitehorned – which had originally belonged to Maeve but had refused to be a woman's property and had joined the king's herd. When Maeve realises this, the rest of her wealth isn't worth a penny to her and she swears to get as good a bull for herself. The only one which is known to be good enough is the black bull of Cooley, owned by a certain Dáire. Maeve immediately sends messengers to Dáire to offer him the most generous terms for the bull, and all goes well until the Connacht emissaries get drunk and are overheard boasting that if the bull were not given freely they would take it by force. Tempers rise, negotiations are broken off, and war is the only possible solution.

It's a human enough incident, very well told in the Book of Leinster, and, when I was preparing a modern Irish version of the Táin for broadcasting some time ago, I couldn't resist including it; but I don't think it's part of the original story. At the very end of the Táin the two bulls, the white one from Connacht and the black one from Ulster, sweep aside the fighting men and finish the war for themselves; the Connacht bull is defeated and the black bull makes his way home triumphantly to Cooley before he, too, dies of his wounds. It is plain that these are no mere animals, but heroic and god-like creatures; we have memories here, however altered, of a cult of bull-gods, such as is well known from the ancient civilisations of the Mediterranean.

The Táin then, like the rest of the Ulster sagas, preserves pre-Christian traditions – but of what period? The German scholar Windisch and the English archaeologist Ridgeway were struck, over fifty years ago, by the resemblances between the chariot-fighting warriors of the Táin and the Celts of Britain and Gaul described by classical writers in the first century B.C., and Windisch pointed out, reasonably enough, that this way of life could have survived considerably longer in Ireland, free from Roman observers and Roman invaders. But, while the Romans seem to have regarded the Gauls as fairly civilised people, the contemporary Irish were not so acceptable; the chariots in the Táin were often decorated with newly acquired human heads, and scholars educated in the classical tradition felt that the Táin stories would be more fittingly placed in a vague and distant past. W. J. Watson, professor of Celtic at Edinburgh, asked 'Would Professor Ridgeway seriously maintain that true Celts (of the first century B.C.), the gentlemen of western Europe, lived in a stage of totemism and polyandry?', and went on to suggest that we might place Cú Chulainn somewhere round 500 B.C. This view lingers on; it is not long since I read an article which said that 'it is an acknowledged fact that the Táin cycle embodies memories of the Celtic way of life and of Celtic beliefs in the centuries from 500 B.C. to 100 A.D.' I think that talking in terms of Celts, and more especially of Celtic gentlemen, is liable to distract our attention from the main point. We know that Celts came to Ireland, since Irish is a Celtic language, and we know that early Irish society has many points in common with that of Celtic Gaul, as well as more distant relationships with early Rome and India. But that Irish society, and the literature it produced, are neither Indo-European nor Celtic, but simply Irish, and must be studied on that basis. Certain elements belonging to the coherent society portrayed in the Táin – totem and tabu, headhunting, fighting from chariots – are unknown in early Christian Ireland and cannot, therefore, be inventions of literary men influenced by Latin learning; we need not go too far in the other direction, however, and regard them as memories of an infinitely remote past. You may remember that some of the antiquarian writers after the end of the Old Irish period like to put the death of Conchobhar Mac Neasa, the King of Ulster in these stories, as coincidental with the death of Christ, but that is, of course, just a conjecture or invention. Remembering that writing was little known in Ireland before the fifth century, and writing in Irish not much before the seventh, we have to ask ourselves how long we should allow for an oral tradition which would preserve all these archaic features, free from any admixture of Christian lore. Not too long, I would suggest; the most important fact that occurs to me is that the same antiquarian writers put the abandonment of Emhain Mhacha, the capital of the Ulstermen in all these tales, somewhere about the middle of the fourth century. It's a common enough device to choose, as the subject of a national epic, a people or kingdom which has no longer any real political existence – it prevents any charges of undue favouritism against the literary men. If the Ulaid, this warlike people who gave their name to the whole province, if they preserved what we might call the Táin way of life up to the fourth century, and then were overwhelmed by an alliance of their enemies, it is not impossible that, just before the coming of Christianity and writing, the stories about them should have become part of the stock-in-trade of the literary men. These stories would hardly have been popular in the first flush of missionary enthusiasm – not popular, that is to say, with the propagators of the new learning. But in no country did the church make its peace with the old learning as quickly or as thoroughly as in Ireland; the elegiac poem in the old bardic style on St. Columba, who died in 597, is sufficient proof that a complete understanding had been arrived at by that date. And I think we might accept one more deduction from the antiquarian writers and say that the alleged finding of the Táin by the poet Seanchán Torpéist in the seventh century – he had to call up Fergus from the dead to tell it – that this finding of the Táin is just the antiquarians' way of saying that it then became respectable to write it down.

Not only writing down this traditional material, but re-arranging it as well. Most of our early sagas are quite short – about the length of this lecture, say. But even the earliest version of the Táin is about ten times that length and the Book of Leinster version longer still; they are no longer stories, but literary works. This, I suppose, was partly due to the fact that the story-tellers now had pen and vellum and could spread themselves, and there's probably a good deal of truth in the suggestion of Thurneysen that the Táin in its present form has been influenced by the Aeneid; the writers were out to provide Ireland with a national epic.

I find that I have been talking as though this seventh century Táin had been preserved, but the fact of the matter is that we can only deduce its existence from later evidence. As you heard from Dr. Dillon in the first lecture, our earliest literary manuscripts in Irish are as late as the twelfth century. One of these, Leabhar na hUidhre, or the Book of the Dun Cow, contains the earliest version of the Táin known to us, and there is another copy of the same version in the Yellow Book of Lecan. But this version is not a straightforward story at all; it is a compilation by somebody who was interested in collecting as much of the varying traditions of the Táin as possible. He does not attempt to conceal the fact; he interjects remarks such as 'They say it is here that Dubhthach sang the lay', 'But other books have the following version', 'According to another version, however', and so on. These are the remarks a modern editor would reserve for footnotes or a preface; here they are jumbled in with the text and, as they suggest, we often find two versions of the same incident told one after the other.

This arises, of course, from the popularity of the story. Once it had been established as the national epic, it became the common property of saga-writers who remoulded it to the taste of their period. We have plenty of parallels from other literature; you will remember

Professor Stanford's researches on the figure of Ulysses throughout the ages, and the play by Giraudoux, called Amphitryon 38, because it was the thirty-eighth handling of the theme, by the dramatist's own reckoning. From this point of view we can regard Yeats's use of Irish saga themes in his verse plays as a perfectly legitimate continuation of a process that had been going on since the beginning of Irish literature. But, to return to the Táin, it is sad that we do not possess one of the early versions in its entirety, instead of having to piece a story together from a very varied material gathered together by the industrious compiler. This piecing together, though, is the sort of job which fascinates scholars, and the great Thurneysen gave us a brilliant analysis; I still have the copy of the text I used as a student, marked in coloured pencils to distinguish Thurneysen's different sources. I won't go into that analysis here, but I must say that a cogent criticism of it was made by Frank O'Connor, on literary rather than academic lines, when he pointed out that the section of the Táin called the *Macgníomhartha,* the 'boyish deeds', must be an interpolation.

The boyish deeds of Cú Chulainn, of course, and no doubt many of you have thought it strange that I have been able to talk so long about the Táin without mentioning the name of the national hero. But, as I have suggested, the original material of the Táin lay in the rivalry between the divine bulls, with which the story still begins and ends; Cú Chulainn's part, originally just an incident in the story, has been enormously expanded, in two ways. The first was to describe, not just one or two of his fights on the ford, while delaying the Connacht troops, but all of them, and in great detail; the most famous of these, the fight with Fer Diad, al-

99

though occurring in the earliest version, is still so late in style and language as to show beyond doubt that it cannot be a great deal older than the twelfth century manuscript in which it is written down. You remember the story: Fer Diad, Cú Chulainn's old friend and comrade, is plied with drink and women, threatened with satire, and cajoled with promises of wealth, until he promises to fight Cú Chulainn, by whom, of course, he falls. Cú Chulainn's lament over him has been well rendered by Sigerson:

'Every other combat and fight that ever I have made was to me but a game or a sport, compared to the combat and the fight of Ferdia:

> Play was each, pleasure each,
> Till Ferdia faced the beach...'

This is fine stuff, as is the quarrel between Ailill and Maeve to which I have already referred, but it is not part of the original story, and neither, in all probability, are most of the fights on the ford, the best of which are by the same hand as wrote the 'boyish deeds' – the Prose-writer, as O'Connor calls him because, though his language is much older than that of the Fer Diad episode, it is not interspersed either with verse or with rhetorics – those passages in obscure alliterative rhythmic language which are characteristic of the older sagas and which we find in long passages between Ailill, Maeve and Fergus in the Táin. The language is barer here and the background more barbarous; take the death of Etarcomol, who forces a fight on Cú Chulainn against Fergus's advice:

Loeg said to Cú Chulainn: 'The chariot is back again and it has turned its left side to us.' 'That is not an obligation that can be refused,' said Cú Chulainn, 'we will go down to the ford to meet it and see about it.' 'I do not wish what you ask of me,' said Cú Chulainn. 'You must do it,' said Etarcomol. Cú Chulainn cut the sod from under his foot, so that he fell with the sod on his belly. 'Get away from me,' said Cú Chulainn, 'I don't want to have to clean my hands on your account. I would have you cut into many pieces long ago had it not been for Fergus.' 'We will not part this way,' said Etarcomol, 'I will bring away your head or leave my head with you.' 'That is what will happen,' said Cú Chulainn and struck with his sword under his two armpits, so that his clothes fell off him but his skin was not touched. 'Go away now,' said Cú Chulainn. 'No,' said Etarcomol. Cú Chulainn swept him then with the edge of his sword and took his hair off as though it had been shaved with a razor. And, since the boor was still tiresome and persistent, he struck him on the top of the head and split him to the navel.

We can imagine how popular this murderous sort of slap-stick was with early Irish audiences, especially when connected with the great name of Cú Chulainn, and they were given plenty of it. But the second and greater triumph of the Prose-writer was his introduction of the stories of the hero's boyhood, given as the reminiscences of Fergus and the other Ulster exiles with Connacht forces – exiles, you will remember, since the death of Deirdre and the sons of Uisliu. This is the technique familiar to us in the modern cinema as the 'flashback', and it is used here with remarkable effect, with little naturalistic touches such as 'that took place in the presence of Bricriu here', and 'I met him in the door of the lios and I badly wounded' and 'nine of the boys dashed past Conchobhar and myself, who were playing chess'. It is more than a little surprising to find so sophisticated a style allied to very primitive, not to say barbarous material; the language of these stories shows that they can hardly have been written much before the ninth century, but there is no admixture at all of classical or ecclesiastical elements. They are one of the happiest examples of the process I have mentioned before, the remoulding of a traditional theme; extraneous though they may be to the action of the Táin, they came to form an integral part of it – indeed, to modern taste, by far the most attractive part. I am sure they are familiar to you; you will remember the picture of the little boy, Sétanta, invited by the king to Culann's feast, for example:

'I haven't had enough of my game yet, uncle Conchobhar,' said the boy, 'I will go after you.' When they all reached the feast Culann said to Conchobhar, 'Is anyone coming after you?' 'No,' said Conchobhar; he did not remember that he had told his foster-son to follow him. 'I have a fierce dog,' said Culann, 'there are three chains on it, and three men on each chain. Let it be loosed to protect our cattle and let the lios be closed.' The boy comes along then. The dog makes for him. He kept on his game meanwhile; he was throwing his ball and throwing his hurling stick after it so that it struck the ball. This shocked Conchobhar and his people so that they were unable to move; they thought they could not reach him alive, even if the lios had been open. When the hound reached him, he threw away his ball and stick and seized the hound with his two hands, one on its throat and the other at the back of its head, and swung it against a pillar-stone which was nearby, so that every limb of it sprang asunder. The Ulstermen rushed towards him, some over the wall, others through the door of the lios, and he was placed in Conchobhar's arms. They raised a great clash of arms, because the son of the king's sister had nearly been killed.

Well, the smith comes along then, and while rejoicing over the boy's escape, laments the death of the dog which protected his wealth, and Sétanta offers to take its place until another dog can be reared; and Cath-bhadh, the druid, says 'Cú Chulainn shall be your name.'

A simple, well-told story, in which the scholars have looked for deeper meanings; Baudiš suggested that the story originally told how Cú Chulainn received his in-dividual totem, the dog – we are told elsewhere that the flesh of the dogs was tabu to him – but O'Rahilly re-jected this as 'learned nonsense', and explained the in-cident as the Hero killing the God. No doubt there is a myth somewhere in the background but the Prose-writer preferred to leave such matters alone; he's care-ful, for example, to suppress the old story that Cú Chu-lainn was the son of the god Lugh. But he had a fine eye for incident and a wonderful feeling for language, and it's a great pity that he didn't do a prose revision of the whole Táin, or if he did, that it has been lost.

For the Táin, taken as a whole, can hardly be called an artistic success; if it's really intended as an imita-tion of the Aeneid, it's a very bad one. Of course, we have to make allowances for the fact that the earliest version we possess is the merest hotch-potch; how much we would give for a sight of those *alii libri,* those other books to which the compiler so often refers! But, even to the present day, the native genius has felt more at home with short stories than with long works of complicated construction; certainly there is nothing in the fragmentary Táin we have that would allow us to suspect the existence of a planned and developed prose epic – nothing to suggest that the Táin was ever otherwise than jerky and episodic. I have suggested that later revisers threw the original story of the contest between the two bulls considerably out of proportion by devoting more and more attention to the attractive figure of the hero Cú Chulainn. And yet the Táin ends, as it begins, with the bulls, with the picture of the Black Bull of Cooley making his way home from Connacht with the carcase of his broken rival on his horns.

VIII

TOGAIL BRUIDNE DA DERGA

By Máirín O Daly

The tale entitled 'The Destruction of Da Derga's Hostel' has perhaps attracted the attention of scholars more than has any other of our saga-stories with the exception of the great epic-tale Táin Bó Cúailnge. Thurneysen, in his study of Irish saga-literature, *Die irische Helden- und Königsage,* shows that the version that survives of the Destruction of Da Derga's Hostel was the handiwork of that same compiler who worked on the Táin.

The oldest version of the tale as we have it is a compilation of the eleventh century based on two earlier versions. Besides this there remains to us a short summary which is preserved in four manuscripts, two of which name the *Cín Dromma Snechta* as source. This *Cín Dromma Snechta* named from Druim Snechta or Drumsnat in Co. Monaghan is a lost manuscript which is believed to have been written in the first half of the eighth century, so that the story was written down at least as early as that date.

Like the Táin, the Destruction of Da Derga's Hostel is the principal tale of a cycle of tales which begins with the lovely story of 'The Wooing of Étaín', which was dealt with by Professor Dillon in the opening talk of this series. But the Táin was an Ulster tale, while the Destruction of Da Derga's Hostel belongs to Leinster. It is true that we find playing a part in it several heroes of the Ulster cycle, but these have been artifically introduced and do not belong to the original version. Its theme is the death of Conaire, King of Tara, when the hostel of Da Derga, in which he was passing the night, was attacked and destroyed by a band of marauders. In the story, magic and other-world personages play a far greater part than they do in the Táin, and indeed the whole tone of the story is very different. Lucius Gwynn once called this cycle 'a group of legends so strangely different in their fatalistic spirit to the later heroic saga that one is tempted to read into them the tradition of a sudden overthrow of an ancient order of things. That the slaying of Conaire, King of Ireland, in Da Derga's Hostel was not merely an interesting legend but as an event had left a deep mark on tradition, is clear from the place it takes in the annals, which after this event record without explanation a gap of five years in the succession of kings.' The story called 'The Wasting Sickness of Cú Chulainn' relates that the men of Ireland were without a king for seven years after the death of Conaire.

Gwynn's theory that this is the tale of the 'sudden overthrow of an ancient order of things' is taken further by O'Rahilly who conjectures in his 'Early Irish History and Mythology' that 'the Destruction of Da Derga's Hostel' is the account of the successful Laginian invasion of the third century B.C. as preserved in the legends of the Érainn – the defeated people – while the tale known as 'The Slaughter of Dinn Ríg', tells the same story from the point of view of the invaders. In 'The Slaughter of Dinn Ríg' the leader of the invading forces, Labraid Loingsech, is the hero, while in 'the Destruction of Da Derga's Hostel' the sympathies of the story-teller are all with Conaire.

Conaire was the son of a woman called Mess Buachalla, a name which means 'the herdsmen's fosterling' for she, a king's daughter, abandoned as a baby at the wish of her stepmother, had been found and reared by the herdsmen of Eterscéle, King of Tara. The King, hearing of her great beauty, took her as his wife. But he was not Conaire's father, for Mess Buachalla was pregnant before her marriage to the King by a man who had appeared to her, coming first in the form of a bird, and had said 'You will bear me a son, and that son may not kill birds, and Conaire shall be his name.'

When the King, Eterscéle, dies, the men of Ireland declare a bull-feast. The feast is thus described: 'They would kill a bull and one man would eat his fill of it and would drink its broth, and an incantation would be chanted over him. The man whom he should see in his sleep, he should be king, but were the sleeper to tell a lie he should die.' This rite, it may be noted, appears to be the one called *Imbas forosnai* (knowledge that illuminates) described by Cormac mac Cuillennáin Kingbishop of Cashel, in his glossary written about 900 A.D. Cormac goes on to say that this incantation was forbidden by Patrick because it was accompanied by sacrifice to demons.

On this occasion the sleeper at the bull-feast sees a naked man carrying a stone in a sling, coming after nightfall along the road to Tara.

Just at this time Conaire is in his chariot in the plain of Life, that is, the plain lying south of the river now called by that name. He pursues a flock of strange birds as far as the sea where they alight on the water. He tries to lay hands on them. The birds throw off their bird-skins, change into human form and attack him with spears and swords. One man of them protects him and says to him 'I am Nemglan, King of your father's bird-flocks and it is forbidden to you to shoot at birds, for there is none here that is not kin to you through his father or his mother.' Then the bird-man counsels him to go to Tara where the bull-feast is being held.

Conaire goes to Tara, naked as he had followed the birds into the water. On each of the four great roads leading to Tara there are kings waiting and they have clothing for him. The people of Tara however are not pleased at the coming of a beardless boy. 'A young, generous king is no reproach,' Conaire says to them. 'It is my right from father and grandfather to bind the hostages of Tara. I shall enquire of wise men so that I myself may be wise.' These things he says as he had been taught by the bird-man who had also foretold to him: 'Your reign will be honoured and the bird-reign will be distinguished, and these will be your prohibitions always:

You shall not go righthandwise round Tara or lefthandwise round Brega.

The *claenmíla* of Cerna shall not be hunted by you (it is not clear what type of animal the *claenmíla* were).

You shall not remain out of Tara on any ninth night.

You shall not sleep in a house out of which the light of a fire is visible after sunset and into which one can see from without.

Three red men shall not go before you to the house of a red man.

A band of marauders shall not land in your reign.

A company consisting of one man or one woman shall not come into the house where you are after sunset.

You shall not restrain a quarrel between two of your serfs.'

In a story probably of the eighth century entitled 'Of the race of Conaire Mór, there is no mention of Conaire's connection with birds and only one prohibition is laid on him, and that by the men of Tara, namely 'That the sun should neither set nor rise on him in Tara.' It is interesting to note that in the life of the sixth century Saint Ruadán we read that the King of Ireland, Diarmait mac Fergusa Cerrbéoil, went out of the city at sunrise because it was *geis*, that is a prohibition, to the rulers of Tara that sunrise should find them within its seven walls.

The reign of Conaire was one of peace and prosperity. The story relates: 'So great was the harmony that existed that no man slew another in Ireland in his reign, and to every man the voice of his fellow was sweet as harpstrings. No wind tossed the hair of cows from the middle of spring to the middle of autumn. His reign was not thundery or stormy.'

But all this comes to an end through the wrongdoing of Conaire's fostersons, the sons of Donn Désa. They thieve three thefts from the one man, a pig, a calf and a cow every year to see what punishment the King would inflict on them for it and what harm thieving in his reign would cause to the King. Finally, after they had in their arrogance formed robber-bands from among the princes' sons, all are captured and brought before the King. Conaire's first impulse is to condemn all to death except his fostersons, but realising how unjust is this judgment, he banishes all from Ireland.

They put to sea and meet with Ingcél Caech son of the King of the Britons. At his suggestion they make a pact – that they should with his aid make a marauding expedition into his country, and that he should make a raid into Ireland with their support. It happened that, in the raid into Britain, Ingcél's father, mother, seven brothers and the king of his district were slain. This does not appear to have grieved him, but he later uses it to strengthen his hand against his allies. The two bands of marauders then return to Ireland to seek an opportunity for the plunder promised to Ingcél.

Meanwhile Conaire had gone south to Thomond to settle a dispute between two of his serfs. This he did though it was forbidden to him, and here begins the violation of one *geis* or prohibition after another which foreshadows his death. He stays five nights with each, thus breaking another *geis*. Returning to Tara he sees as it were the plain of Meath overrun by invaders and the land around Tara seemed all on fire. To avoid it he turns north-east, and breaks two more of his *gessa* by going righthandwise round Tara and lefthandwise round the plain of Brega and by unwittingly hunting the *claenmíla* of Cerna. He turns south along the coast and decides to pass the night in the hostel of Da Derga, a friend on whom he had bestowed many gifts and who would surely welcome him.

Journeying south along the road called Slige Cúalann he sees before him three horsemen. Both riders and horses are red. Conaire, recognising that this again is the violation of a *geis*, that three red men should go before him to the house of a red man, that is, the house of Da Derga, sends his son to ask them not to go before the King. Three times the son spurs his horse after them but in vain; they remain a spear-cast ahead, and each time one of them chants over his shoulder a chant which portends slaughter. The last chant goes: 'Lo, o son, great the tidings. Weary are the horses we ride. We ride the horses of Donn Desschorach from the fairy mounds. Though we are alive we are dead. Great the cuttings-off of lives. Sating of ravens. Sustenance of ravens. Din of slaughter. In the hours after sunset blades hack the edges of broad-bossed shields.' The three red men ride on, and a sense of foreboding comes upon Conaire and his troops. 'All my *gessa* have seized upon me tonight,' says Conaire.

At the hostel Da Derga welcomes him saying 'Though the greater part of the men of Ireland were with you, I would feed them.'

A hideous hag comes to the door and foretells the slaying of Conaire. She demands hospitality and, in spite of his *geis* not to receive after sunset a company consisting of one man or one woman, he allows her to enter.

The hostel lay so that the river Dodder flowed through the house. There were seven doorways in it but only one door, and this was placed in whichever doorway the wind blew upon.

Meanwhile the marauders headed by the sons of Donn Désa and Ingcél Caech have landed. On their way from the seashore they halt to take counsel at a spot from which the light of the fire in the hostel can be seen shining through the wheels of the chariots drawn up before the open doors.

Ingcél goes to spy out the hostel and through the six open doors he sees and notes the appearance and characteristics of the occupants of the many apartments. He does not of course know who they are. He returns to his companions. All gather round to hear his account of what he has seen. 'The arrangement is kingly,' he says, 'the clamour is indicative of a host, its sound is princely. Whether there be a king there or not, I shall accept the plunder of the house in payment of what is due to me.'

Then Ingcél describes in turn the occupants of each apartment of the hostel and each time Fer Rogain, one of Conaire's fostersons, identifies them and foretells what slaughter each will inflict on the attackers and whether he will survive the battle. This device of describing personages of the story not directly but through the mouth of one who has observed them but does not know them is used also in the Táin. There Mac Roth the messenger is sent by Ailill to spy out the advancing army of the Ulstermen, and returning he describes what he has seen. Then Fergus, himself an Ulsterman but now fighting on the side of Ailill and Medb, identifies each one. Again, you will remember from Professor O'Brien's account of Bricriu's Feast, how Findabair the daughter of Ailill and Medb, looking out from the *grianán* before her parents' court, describes three Ulster warriors who are approaching in their chariots, and Medb names each one from the description. Some scholars have seen in this the influence of that passage in the third book of the Iliad where Helen, looking down from the walls of Troy on the Grecian warriors in the plain below, identifies for King Priam, who questions her, Agamemnon, Ajax and Ulysses. But the resemblance between the incidents to me seems so slight as not to furnish sufficient grounds for believing that the Irish story-teller had borrowed from the Greek.

To return to our story; on each occasion when Fer Rogain has named the warrior or warriors described by Ingcél, Lomna the Jester, another of the fostersons, interjects 'Alas for him who wreaks the slaughter. If my advice might prevail, the slaughter would not be attempted,' but on each occasion Ingcél retorts 'You do not prevail.'

At last Ingcél calls on the attackers to rise up and approach the house. They arise and utter their war-cry, Lomna the Jester first enters the hostel and is, as he himself has foretold, the first to die. Three times the

house is set on fire and three times the fire is quench-
ed. Conaire inflicts great slaughter, and the attackers
are driven back. Fer Rogain tells them that unless Conaire's ardour and valour be destroyed their attack will
fail. The druids who accompany the marauders by their
magic power bring an exhausting thirst on Conaire
who returns to the house and asks for a drink. But all
the drink in the house has been thrown on the flames,
and his cupbearers can find no water for him in the
Dodder which, as you recall, flows through the house.
Finally, his champion, Mac Cécht, unwillingly leaves
the fight and visits all the rivers and lakes of Ireland
seeking a drink for his lord. All hide their waters from
him until he reaches Uarán Garaid in Roscommon
which cannot hide from him.

As he approaches the hostel on his return, two men
are striking off the head of Conaire. Mac Cécht slays
both and pours the water he has brought into Conaire's
headless neck. The severed head speaks 'Excellent is
Mac Cécht, good is Mac Cécht, who brings a drink to a
king and performs a deed of valour.'

There are other instances in the saga literature of a
severed head speaking. In the Battle of Allen the severed head of Donn Bó sings to his dead lord on the battle-
field, for the night before he had promised: 'Wherever
you may be tomorrow night, I will entertain you.' In the
Táin, Sualdam's head repeats after death the warning
that in life went unheeded.

The story ends with Conall Cernach's return from the
battle to his father's house.

The element of tragedy in this tale has struck all who
have studied it. Battle and violent death are common-
places of our sagas as they are of the heroic tales of
all peoples. In the story of the death of Cú Chulainn also,

a succession of broken *gessa* leads up dramatically to the hero's death, but there is no feeling of sadness, rather of exultation. Cú Chulainn dies as he would have expected and desired, and as Oliver Sheppard's fine statue in the G.P.O. portrays him, sword in hand facing his enemies on whom he has inflicted great slaughter. He dies merely because at last the odds against him are too great. The case of Conaire is different. He too is a warrior. But he is primarily a king, a ruler, and so might have looked forward to dying a peaceful death, old and honoured. Dr. Eleanor Knott speaks of 'a young king foredoomed to a tragic death to which he is relentlessly urged on by fate, his kindliest deeds entangling him most inextricably in the mesh,' and O'Rahilly has described Conaire as 'an innocent victim of relentless fate'. There is, however, another way of looking at these incidents. Conaire's fate was brought about, not by his successive and sometimes unwitting violations of all his *gessa* but by the one act of injustice of which he was guilty – his condemning to death the companions in rapine and plunder of his three fostersons and his sparing the latter although they were the leaders of the robber-bands. So well-beloved was he that his people, even the fathers of the condemned accepted his unjust judgment without a murmur but he himself recognised its injustice and revoked it. 'Let each one kill his son,' he had said, 'but let my fosterlings be spared.' All agreed, but then he added 'Nay, then. The judgment I have given is no extension of life to me,' and he ordered that the lives of all should be spared but that all should be banished.

Throughout our early literature great stress is laid on the necessity for justice in the ruler. In 'The Instructions of Morand' (Morand was a famous judge) we read: 'As long as the prince preserves justice no good thing will be lacking from him and his rule will not perish,' and, continuing, the text enumerates the many advantages that spring from the justice of the ruler – peace, fruitful harvests, the warding-off of pestilences, etc. In the tale called 'The Battle of Mag Mucraime', of which you will hear later from Professor Carney, Lugaid Mac Con, though a usurper, reigned prosperously in Tara for seven years, but at the end of that time he delivered an unjust judgment, and the story goes: 'For a year after that he was in kingship in Tara and no grass came through the ground, nor leaf through trees, nor grain into corn. Then the men of Ireland rejected him from his kingship because he was a false prince.'

Conaire appears in the story as a young king. Outside the story, however, tradition gives him a long reign. According to the Lebor Gabála and the Four Masters he reigned for seventy years, according to the Annals of Clonmacnoise for sixty years. Keating writes 'Conaire Mór... held the sovereignty of Ireland thirty years, or according to others seventy years.' The peace and prosperity of his reign became a legend and this would seem more likely of a long reign. It has been suggested that some story-teller represented Conaire as a young king in order to heighten the tragedy of his death. I would suggest that it was not to heighten it but to explain it. The story as handed down already carries a heavy burden of tragedy. When the fact that it told not only the death of a king but the end of a dynasty and the subjugation of a people was forgotten, the reason for this tragedy was not apparent. Such grief at even the violent death of an aged king would seem excessive, for we must remember that, unrealistic in many things, our early story-tellers were quite otherwise in everything that pertained to human relations and emotions.

Another element that adds to the pathos of Conaire's death is the presence among his attackers of his foster-sons whom he had loved even to the point of committing an injustice for their sake, and whom, although he had banished them from Ireland, he still desires to see. A note of bitter irony is introduced when the marauders reach the shore. The story goes: 'They come to land. The noise the three fifties of currachs made in running ashore shook Da Derga's hostel so that there was not left a spear upon a rack but they all made a clatter and fell upon the floor of the house.'

'Say, what noise is this, Conaire?' he is asked.

'I have nothing to compare with it,' he replies 'unless it be the ground which has turned over, or unless it be the Leviathan which encircles the earth that has struck with its tail to overturn the world, or the boat of the sons of Donn Désa which has come to land. Alas that it is not they! They were our beloved fosterlings. Dear was the warrior band. We should have no fear of them tonight.' And while he speaks thus lovingly of them, they are drawing near and are about to attack him.

Again the emotional impact is intensified by the attitude of the sons of Donn Désa. Had they come willingly to aid in the attack on their fosterfather the tragedy would not have been so poignant. But evildoers as they were, they recognised his goodness and did not desire his death. One of them, Fer Rogain, when asked by Ingcél 'What are the characteristics of that man's rule in Ireland?' answers: 'His rule is good' and goes on to speak of the peace and prosperity of his reign, adding: 'May God not bring that man here tonight. It were grievous that shortness of life should come to him.' But the fostersons were bound by contract to Ingcél Caech, who was determined to have a fitting prey, and he rejoins: 'It would be most satisfying to me that it should be he. It would not seem to me more grievous than my mother and my father and my seven brothers and the king of my district that I gave to you.'

The eleventh-century compiler who produced the version of the story that survives had as his aim the combining of the two ninth-century versions that lay before him but, over-anxious to preserve every tradition, he did not edit his material skilfully, and he has left us a tale full of inconsistencies and repetitions. He has not however succeeded in depriving it of that enchantment that must have been even more striking in some earlier version. There is, as in many other tales, a strange mixture of conciseness and prolixity, realism and fantasy; conciseness and realism in the conversations of which there are many, prolixity and fantasy in the descriptive passages. The descriptions are very similar to, but often more elaborate than those in other tales. That wonderful description of Étaín with which the story opens and which Professor Dillon read for you in the first talk of this series is the most detailed description of a woman in early Irish literature and has something in common with that of the prophetess Fedelm in the beginning of the Táin Bó Cúailnge. With the account of the army of Conchobar mac Nessa as given by Mac Roth in the Táin we may compare that of the followers of Conaire in the hostel given by Ingcél. To a modern reader these repetitive descriptions may seem tedious, but they must have seemed quite otherwise to the listening audience when recited with skill and artistry. Thurneysen remarks, perhaps a little critically, that as the incidents of the battle are foretold in the account of Conaire's followers, when the battle actually begins there is no more to tell. But in reality the foretelling of the slaughter and the consequent shortening of the later account is more effective than would have been a longer description of the battle as it took place, and it is a remarkable fact that the Irish story-teller, whose material so often consisted of battles, deals with them in a very sketchy and often a very unrealistic way. It is clear that to him and his audience the portraying of character and the conveying of emotion were of first importance.

The final passage of the story, the meeting between Conall Cernach and his father Amorgein, will illustrate this emotional appeal and end this talk:

Conall has come grievously wounded from the hostel and finds his father before the door of his court in Tailtiu.

'Swift are the hounds that have hunted you, little son,' said his father. 'Have you news of Da Derga's hostel? Is your lord alive?'

'He is not alive,' said Conall.

'I swear to the god to whom my people swear, it is cowardly for the man who came away alive having left his lord with his enemies in death.'

'Nevertheless my wounds are not white, old warrior,' said Conall. Then he showed his shield-arm which though partly protected by the shield had received three times fifty wounds, while the right arm was so hacked and wounded that only the sinews still held it to the body.

'That arm fought tonight, little son, and was fought against,' said Amorgein.

'That is true, old warrior,' said Conall Cernach, 'Many are they to whom a drink of death was given tonight before the Hostel.'

IX

ACALLAM NA SENÓRACH

By Gerard Murphy

Finn Mac Cool, in classical Irish Finn mac Cumaill which means Finn son of Cumall, is one of the few figures of ancient Irish tradition who has survived the decay of the Irish language and whose name is still familiar to Irishmen of every rank of life all over Ireland. Often he is remembered as a giant responsible for certain local landmarks. A lake is explained as a hollow made in the land by him when he scooped out a handful of earth to throw at an enemy. A long grassy spot on a rough mountainside may be said to have once been his bed. A well-known rock is a missile used by him to slay a rival giant; and so on. These traditions are remnants of the Finn of folklore and ancient mythology. They are even older than the many tales and ballads of Irish literature which depict Finn as a human hero with certain magic attributes, a warrior-hunter with the power of second sight, obtained through chewing his magic thumb, or through laying his thumb under a magic tooth which he possessed.

The famous story of Diarmuit and Gráinne belongs to a certain extent to the two traditions. It tells how Gráinne, betrothed to Finn, eloped with Finn's younger follower, Diarmuit. Since Irish has ceased to be the common literary language of Ireland, the literary story of Diarmuit and Gráinne has ceased to be a houehold tale known to every Irish man and woman. But the ancient mythological traditions on which the literary tale was based survive more or less in the explanation of certain local landmarks as sleeping-places of the lovers, and in the almost universal description of what archaeologists call dolmens as 'beds of Diarmuit and Gráinne'.

Already well before the twelfth century of our era learned men in Ireland had composed literary tales concerning Finn's wooing of Gráinne and Gráinne's subsequent elopement with Diarmuit. Similar men of learning in our native schools of history had also been making up their minds as to who Finn really was. Everyone, they argued, knew of Finn. Unlettered people could tell folktales about him. A place therefore should be found for him in that vast scheme of pseudo-history which had gradually been worked out in the native schools between the eighth century and the twelfth. The teachers in these native schools of history ultimately reached the conclusion that Finn had been captain of the professional soldiery of Cormac, king of Tara, in the middle of the third century of our era. His Fian, the band of hunter-warriors with whom ancient tradition had always associated him, were actually identified by these medieval Irish scholars as Cormac's professional soldiery.

About the beginning of the twelfth century, that, then, is how matters stood. Finn was a character known to everyone by reason of his popularity with tellers of folktales and by reason of mythological memories connecting him with local landmarks. He had received a new status among men of learning by reason of the two or three literary adaptations already in existence of the old mythological traditions concerning the elopement of Gráinne, and above all by a place being found for him as a human warrior-captain with a date in the third century and human historical associations.

Now, all over Europe, the twelfth century was a century of intellectual, ecclesiastical, and social development. It was the century of Peter Abélard in the university, of St. Bernard in the history of monasticism, and of the emperor Frederick Barbarossa in European politics. A similar spirit of growth and innovation was manifesting itself in the twelfth century in Ireland. High-Kings were beginning to exercise authority in the domains of local kings, after the manner of national monarchs. Churches were being built in the new Hiberno-Romanesque style. Church government was being drastically reformed. The manuscripts on which our knowledge of Old and Middle Irish literature is largely based were being compiled. The great Irish epic tale known as *Táin Bó Cúailnge* (The Cattle-Raid of Cooley) was being retold in a new style. Classical epic tales such as the Aeneid were being adapted from Latin for the Irish story-loving public.

For the innovators of the twelfth century, Finn Mac Cumaill and his Fian, had a special attraction. They were well-known figures of tradition who had recently received literary and historical status. Their literary tradition was not, however, firmly fixed by age-old literary custom, as was the case with Cú Chulainn and the Ulidian heroes of the heroic tradition, or with the Kings of the kingly tradition of storytelling. Finn and his Fian therefore offered possibilities of development in new ways.

Ballads, that is to say short narrative poems in stanzaic form, intended to be sung, were becoming popular in western Europe in the early twelfth century. It was untraditional in the old literary cycles of Ireland – the Cú Chulainn cycle, the King cycle, and the mythological cycle – to use verse for pure narration. The Irish in those old cycles had always used prose for pure narration, in-

terspersing the prose with occasional verse in the form
of prophetic utterances, of laments or of other expres-
sions of emotion. When the innovators of the twelfth
century wished therefore to introduce the new genre of
balladry into Ireland they introduced it into the Finn
cycle where no age-old literary custom imposed a
fixed form on men of letters. And, from the twelfth
century on, a rich ballad literature was composed in
Ireland, confined almost wholly to the adventures of
Finn and his Fian.

Similarly when, towards the end of the twelfth century, some unknown Irishman of genius, steeped in the
ancient lore of Ireland, but inspired also by the innovat-
ing tendencies of his time, got the idea of combining all
the modes and spirits of the various branches of Irish
tradition in one vast new literary compilation, he turned
to the Finn cycle as the cycle in which such a combination of antiquity and innovation might most fittingly be
attained. He entitled his compilation *Acallam na Senórach,* which is usually translated The Colloquy of the
Ancient Men.

Nothing quite like *Acallam na Senórach* exists elsewhere in Irish literature. Yet, on the other hand, nothing
so typically Irish is to be found elsewhere in Irish. In it
folk-motifs, mythological motifs, warrior motifs, *sen-
chus* (that is to say 'history') motifs, *dinn-shenchus*
(that is to say 'place-lore') motifs, lyric poetry, ballad
poetry, and learned poetry, are found harmoniously
united in a single whole; and that whole is cast in the
form of a romantic *dinn-shenchus,* or place-history, of
Ireland, a genre of learned literature which had for long
been popular.

Acallam na Senórach has been preserved for us in
various fragments of slightly different versions, which,

when compared with one another, give us an almost complete picture of the original whole. I shall not weary you here by discussing those various fragments and versions in detail. Readers of Irish will find a full account of them in the Introduction to the three-volume edition of *Agallamh na Seanórach,* published by Nessa Ní Shéaghdha, between 1942 and 1945. The text of Nessa Ní Shéaghdha's version is comparatively late one; and the text usually referred to by Irish scholars is that edited by Standish Hayes O'Grady in the first volume of his *Silva Gadelica* published in 1892, or that published by Whitley Stokes in 1900, using different manuscripts. Readers of English will find an excellent English translation of that text in the second volume of Standish Hayes O'Grady's *Silva Gadelica.*

The Acallam opens with a pseudo-historical paragraph, which may be translated as follows into English:

After the Battle of Comar and the Battle of Gabair and the Battle of Ollarba had been fought, and the Fian had almost been annihilated, they scattered in groups and bands over Ireland so that at the moment of which we speak only two leading warriors of the remnants of the Fian survived, namely Oisín son of Finn, and Caílte son of Crunnchu son of Rónán, with their strength and agility decayed. They were accompanied by two groups of nine warriors each; and those two groups came out of the borders of the flowery-soiled wooded Fews Mountains and moved on to Lugbairt Bána (or White Gardens) which are today known as Lugbad (or Louth), and they were gloomy and dispirited there as the clouds of evening fell that night. Then Caílte said to Oisín: 'Well now, beloved Oisín, what road should we take before the end of the day to seek entertainment for the night?' 'I know not,' said Oisín. 'since of the ancients of the Fian and of the former followers of Finn mac Cumaill only three survive, namely myself, you and Caílte, and Cáma, the female chief and female custodian who watched over Finn mac Cumaill from the time he was a child up to the day on which he died.'

The original Irish of that paragraph is as straightforward as the English translation of it I have read for you; but it would be difficult to give in English the effect of the alliterations of the original, and of the high-sounding adjectives deliberately chosen by the author to suit public recitation of the story before a gathering in some Irish sub-king's hall in the late twelfth century. The slightly awkward English phrase 'out of the borders of the flowery-soiled wooded Fews Mountains' fails almost completely, for instance, to suggest the perfection of the alliterating Irish *a himlib Sléibe Fuait fonnscothaig foithremail,* and the same is true of many other phrases scattered richly through this paragraph and other paragraphs which will be quoted later. The citation of a fictitious or genuine old name, *Lugbairt Bána* (White Gardens), for modern *Lugbad* or Louth, is another trait designed to please a twelfth-century Irish audience accustomed to think highly of *dinn-shenchus* or place-lore.

The paragraph I have read for you is followed by an episode in which the two ancient warriors decide to repair to Cáma's house, where they were entertained generously for three days and three nights, talking over the past and lamenting the friends who had gone from them. On the next morning Caílte and Oisín left Cáma's homestead, and, to return to quotation from the *Acallam* itself,

coming out upon the grassy green they took counsel, and the plan they decided on was to part with one another; and that parting was as the parting of soul with body. And, following their plan, Oisín went to the Fairy Mound of Ucht Cleitig, where his mother Blaí daughter of Derg Dianscothach dwelt, while Caílte went ahead to the Estuary of Bec Loingsech in Brega, which is called the Monastery of Drogheda today... From that he went to Linn Fhéic on the white-streamed Boyne, and southwards over the Old Plain of Brega to the Fort of Druim Derg, where Patrick son of Calpurnius happened then to be.

There Patrick was chanting the divine office and praising the Creator, and blessing the fort in which was Finn son of Cumall, that is to say, the Fort of Druim Derg. And the clerics saw the warriors approaching, and they were filled with horror and fear of the huge men accompanied by their huge hounds, for they were not people of one epoch or of one time with the clergy.

And then the Salmon of Authority, and the Pillar of Lordship, and the Earthly Angel, known as Patrick son of Calpurnius, Apostle of the Irish, seized a sprinkler to shake holy water upon the huge men, for a thousand legions of devils had been hovering over them up to that day; and the devils went into the hills and clefts and edges of that region and territory, scattering in every direction. Thereupon the huge men sat down.

Having thus brought the pagan warriors of the third century and the Christian missionaries of the fifth into contact with one another, the author of the *Acallam* goes on to describe their friendly converse or Colloquy as they journeyed over Ireland together, ultimately meeting Oisín too, who comes forth from his mother's fairy hill. In the course of the Colloquy over two hundred anecdotes and tales of the past are related. The first of these occurs almost immediately after the meeting of Caílte and Patrick. It tells how Caílte led Patrick to a spring-well suitable for baptising the peoples of North Dublin and Meath. Like many of the anecdotes its beauty is enhanced by inclusion of a short poem in pleasantly rhymed verse. For, according to the author of the *Acallam*, Caílte, having shown Patrick the well, began to tell its fame and qualities in the following poem:

Well of Tráig Dá Ban,
lovely is your pure-topped cress;
since your verdure has become neglected
no growth has been allowed to your brooklime.

Your trout out by your banks,
your wild swine in your wilderness,
the deer of your crags fine for hunting,
your dappled red-bellied fawns.

Your mast on the tips of your trees,
your fish in the mouths of your streams,
lovely is the colour of your sprigs of arum lily,
green brook in the wooded hollow!*

After Caílte had uttered that poem, we are told by

126

the author of the *Acallam* how the warriors and the clerics dined together. The meal was followed by conversation; and many tales and anecdotes were told, with poems interspersed. This first group of tales and anecdotes of the *Acallam* begins as follows:

'The lord under whom you served,' said Patrick, 'that is to say Finn mac Cumaill, was he a good lord?' And Caílte in reply uttered this little verse of praise:

> 'Were but the brown leaf,
> which the wood sheds from it, gold,
> were but the white billow silver,
> Finn would have given it all away.'

'And what was it that maintained you living thus?' asked Patrick. And Caílte answered: 'Truth that was in our hearts, and strength in our hands, and fulfilment in our tongues.'

Here perhaps we have an echo of the heroic tradition of the old Ulidian stories, in which strength of hand and fulfilment of the plighted word are the most admired virtues.

During the recital of that first night's complement of tales and poems Patrick several times expresses his delight at what he is being told, commonly including in his words of approval the formula *Ad-rae buaid ocus bennacht,* 'May victory and blessing attend you.' Once indeed about the beginning of the night he expresses

* The translation of the poem has been taken from Professor K. Jackson's Studies in Celtic Nature Poetry (1935, 15). The poem has four further quatrains in the original, in which legendary episodes connected with the well are mentioned.

some anxiety concerning the distraction from prayer that this listening to story-telling entails. And in the final phrases of thanks and blessing his anxiety is expressed as follows:

'May victory and blessing attend you, Caílte,' said Patrick; 'all this is recreation of spirit and mind to us, did it not entail destruction of devotion, and neglect of prayer, and abandonment of praise of the Lord.'

Next morning, however, Patrick's doubts were set at rest. For his two guardian angels appeared to him and spoke as follows:

'Beloved holy cleric,' said they, 'those ancient warriors can tell you no more than a third of their stories by reason of forgetfulness and lack of memory. And see to it that what they say be written on poets' staves and in learned men's words, for it will be a delight to gatherings of people and to noblemen in later times to listen to those tales.'

While such of us in these later times as listen to the many stories which Caílte and Oisín told Patrick in the course of the rest of the Colloquy, must miss some of their charm if we cannot hear them in their Irish form and with full appreciation of the twelfth-century mentality which they were originally designed to please, nevertheless summary description of a few of them may succeed in suggesting something of their original excellence.

The story of Cael and Créd told by Caílte to Patrick, at Ard Patrick, Co. Limerick, has rightly been admired more than almost any other part of the Acallam. It opens with a *dinn-shenchus* of Ard Patrick (Patrick's Hill), in which Caílte gives a quaint reason for its once having being called *Finntulach* or the White Hill. Having uttered a poem describing the beauties of the hill, Caílte continues in prose as follows:

And it is from here we went to fight the battle of Ventry. And we saw one of Finn's people approaching us, namely Cael the Valiant, slayer of hundreds, grandson of Nemnann. 'Whence have you come, Cael?' said Finn. 'From dewy Brug na Bóinne in the north,' said Cael. 'What was your errand there?' said Finn. 'I went to consult Muirenn daughter of the Derg, my foster-mother,' said Cael. 'For what reason?' said Finn. 'Because of a fairy lover and noble spouse who appeared in vision to me, namely Créd daughter of white-skinned Cairbre, King of Ciarraige Luachra.'

Finn then asked Cael did he know the conditions on which Créd's hand was to be won. Cael replied that he was aware of them, and had gone to his fairy foster-mother in the magic Brug specially to get help to fulfil them. The conditions were that the wooer had to bring with him a poem which adequately described Créd's marvellous dwelling with all its fittings and furniture. His fairy foster-mother had taught him such a poem.

Finn and the Fian then accompanied Cael to the Paps mountains in north Kerry, beneath which Créd lived. The poem of twenty-three quatrains pleased Créd, and even the following four quatrains of it, quoted in English with loss of the rhyme, metre, and alliteration of the original, will show that Créd had good reason to be pleased.

There are a hundred feet in Créd's house from one
end to the other, and fifty measured feet in breadth
of its good doorway.

Its wattling and its thatch are of the feathers of blue
and yellow birds; its railing beside the well to the
east is of glass and carbuncle.

Around each bed are four pillars of patterned gold
and silver; there is a glass gem on the top of each pillar, crowning it pleasantly.

There is a vat there of princely enamel into which
flows the juice of pleasant malt, and an apple-tree
above the vat with abundance of heavy fruit.

The *Acallam* goes on to describe how the couple were
married and the marriage feast celebrated for a week.
Then all moved on to fight the battle of Ventry against
foreign invaders. On the last day of the battle Cael was
drowned on the shore of Ventry; and the story ends with
an account of Créd's moving lament for her dead husband.

Créd then came and laid herself by his side and
wailed aloud in great sorrow. 'Why should I not die,'
said she, 'of grief for my husband, seeing that the
restless wild creatures are dying of grief for him?'
And she said:

The haven roars over the fierce stream of Reen-
verc: the drowning of the warrior from Loch Dá
Chonn is what the wave striking the shore laments.

Sad is the cry the thrush makes in Drumkeen, and no less sad is the note of the blackbird in Leitir Laíg.

Sad is the sound made by the stag in Drumlesh: dead is the doe of Druim Sílenn; a mighty stag roars now that she has gone.

It is grievous to me that Cael should be dead by my side, and that a wave should have swept over his fair body: the greatness of his beauties set my wits astray.

Sad is the cry made by the shore's wave upon the beach; since it has drowned a fine noble man, it is grievous to me that Cael ever went near it.

And the girl lay down by Cael's side and died of grief for him and they were both buried there in a single tomb; and it is I myself (said Caílte) who raised the stone which is over their grave, so that it is called the Tomb of Cael and Créd.

'Victory and blessing attend you, Caílte,' said Patrick: 'you have told a good story; and where is Brócán the scribe?'

'I am here,' said Brócán.

'Write all that Caílte has said.' And it was written.

The *Acallam,* as we have already seen, succeeds throughout in holding our attention in two ways, first by reason of our interest in the wanderings of Caílte and Oisín and Patrick and in the kings and others with whom they came in contact, secondly by reason of our interest in the stories Caílte tells. When Caílte and Patrick, for instance, were in the neighbourhood of Athy (Co. Kildare), Caílte, in a short anecdote followed by a quatrain of poetry, explained the origin of the placename Fert Raírinne (Raíriu's Mound) to Patrick. The Mound, it would appear, had been called after Caílte's own sister Raíriu, who had died and was buried there.

'And I would like to ask you a request, holy cleric,' continued Caílte. 'What is your request, beloved one?' said Patrick. 'To bring my sister out of torment, seeing that I have become one of your followers and favoured ones.' 'May (she) and your mother and your father and Finn mac Cumaill, your lord, be delivered from torment for your sake,' said Patrick, 'if God wills it.' Caílte gave thanks to Patrick for that, and it is the best gift that Caílte ever got.

A little further on they came to a place called the Garbthanach or Rough Washing. 'Tell us, beloved Caílte,' said Patrick, why this place has been called Rough Washing.' This question of Patrick's gives Caílte the occasion for giving the best telling preserved for us in Irish of the tragic tale of Fithir and Dáirine, the two daughters of Tuathal King of Tara. The king of Leinster, Echaid mac Echach Áinchinn, had come to Tuathal to ask the hand of his younger daughter Fithir in marriage. Tuathal would not give the younger in marriage before the elder, so the king of Leinster had to be content with the elder sister Dáirine. He could not love her, however, so he enclosed her with nine companions in a strong secret dwelling in the midst of the forest and returning to Tuathal, said that she had died. Tuathal then gave him Fithir, the younger sister, whom he had always wanted. After the marriage Fithir accidentally met her elder sister Dáirine. The shock of the meeting caused Fithir's death; and Dáirine, seeing her sister dead before her, died of grief for her. The Rough Washing of their corpses for burial was the cause, according to Caílte, of the name Garbthanach being given to the townland in which they died. 'May victory and blessing attend you, beloved Caílte,' said Patrick; 'it is a good story you have told us.'

As an example of the narrative poetry included in the *Acallam* let me quote for you, before I conclude, some stanzas of a poem uttered by Caílte one snowy first of November when he was with Patrick in the Fews Mountains, Co. Armagh:

Winter is cold; the wind has risen; the fierce stark-wild stag arises; not warm tonight is the unbroken mountain, even though the swift stag be belling.

The stag of Slievecarran of the assemblies does not lay his side to the ground; the stag of the Head of cold Aughty listens likewise to wolf-music.

I thank the King of Heaven, Son of the Virgin Mary: often used I to still armies, though I be tonight very cold.

The end of the *Acallam* is missing in all versions. It probably described how Caílte and Oisín, both previously baptized by Patrick, departed from this world at the festival known as *Feis Temrach* (The feast of Tara). Lovers of medieval literature have reason to be grateful to Patrick's guardian angels for having instructed him to record in *Acallam na Senórach,* before their death, the collection of tales and poems I have described, 'to be a delight to gatherings of people and to noblemen in later times.'

X

TÓRAIGHEACHT DHIARMADA AGUS GHRÁINNE

By R. A. Breatnach

Of all the tales about Fionn mac Cumhaill and the Fiana none is better known than *Tóraigheacht Dhiarmada agus Ghráinne*, 'The Pursuit of Diarmaid and Gráinne'. It was first published with an English translation just under a century ago by Standish Hayes O'Grady in the Transactions of the Ossianic Society for 1855. O'Grady's text and translation have been re-printed several times in the interests of students, and in P. W. Joyce's rendering, published sixty years ago in *Old Celtic Romances*, the tale became known to a wider public. Some of you may have studied the story in your Secondary School days or read about it in textbooks of history or savoured its charm in Mícheál Mac Liammóir's delightful play in Irish. For the reader of modern Irish, and indeed for the reader who had to depend on the translation, the appeal of the tale is immediate. Here is a theme that manifestly belongs to great literature: the story of a tragic love, set in a *milieu* of primeval nature touched with 'that magic of Celtic romance', which Matthew Arnold loved and praised, and elaborated in a peculiar, original style of story-telling redolent of antiquity.

The poignant echo of the protest of the young girl when compelled to marry an old man is sometimes heard in later Irish songs. But the protest is verbal only. In *Tóraigheacht Dhiarmada agus Ghráinne* it is otherwise. But Gráinne was the daughter of Cormac son of Art, son of Conn of the Hundred Battles, High-King of Ireland, and (we are told) she was young and 'the fairest of feature and form and speech of the women of the whole world'. At her father's bidding, she had agreed to marry Fionn mac Cumhaill who was old and a widower. But she loved Fionn's friend and follower, Diarmaid 'of the white teeth and lightsome countenance', the darling of all the women and maidens of Ireland. She determined, at whatever cost, that Diarmaid should carry her off. Forced to betray his friend and leader under pain of infringing more sacred obligations placed on him by Gráinne, Diarmaid is the apotheosis of tragedy as he goes out with her into the night with the words of the seer Diorraing still ringing in his ears: 'I tell you to follow Gráinne, and your death will come of it, and I think it is an evil thing.'

The Ireland in which Diarmaid and Gráinne travel, for all its appearance of reality, for all the solidity of its woods and mountains, is really the land of Irish story-telling. The places all have well-known names, it is true, and are given locations in Ireland, but the reader notices that nearly everyone of them has two names, one fictional and the other historical. For the medieval Irish story-teller was careful to give his tale geographical authentication, just as he sought to give his heroes historicity by providing them with genealogies. The world in which the action of the *Tóraigheacht* takes place, as in all the tales of the Fiana, is an ambivalent one, an amalgam of the real and imagined where the 'Peoples of the Goddess Danu', the Tuatha Dé Danann, have equal rights with the race of men. And why not? They had accepted the Faith from Patrick himself according to the late twelfth century *Acallam na Senó-*

rach; and the fifteenth century *Cath Fionntrágha* records that there was not 'a king's son or a prince's son
or a leader of a band of the Fiana whose wife or mother
or nurse or lover' was not of them. The mother of Fionn
himself, the *Book of Leinster* records, was of this people, who, as we read elsewhere, were only 'another lot
of the men of Ireland who dare not be over ground but
in fairy mansions underground'. In such a world as this
one expects that men should be something more than
human and gods something less than divine.

The tragic concept just outlined of the romance of
Diarmaid and Gráinne deserved to be told in the grand
manner. In fact, it was outside Ireland, in the French
Arthurian cycle of Tristan and Isolde, that the theme,
derived from Celtic sources, reached its highest point
of literary development. This was in the late twelfth
and early thirteenth centuries. In Ireland, although it is
certain that some form of the tale of the elopement of
the lovers and their pursuit by Fionn was in existence
long before this time, we cannot be sure that the story in
the form in which we know it had taken shape until
much later: possibly not before the sixteenth century. It
would be interesting, if we had time, to spend a few
moments with the poets and story-tellers of the tenth and
following centuries in order to trace our theme back to its
literary sources. They have much to tell us of a tale which
seanchaithe of the last generation in Ireland and in Gaelic
Scotland still remembered in outline; a tale of which
cromlechs speak wherever they bear the name *Leaba
Dhiarmada agus Ghráinne*, 'the Bed of Diarmaid and
Gráinne', or *Leaba na Caillighe* 'the Bed of the Hag'
– a strange personage of whom you will hear later on.
But you will wish to know what the *Pursuit* is about
rather than what its literary origins are. It is not an

easy matter to summarize it satisfactorily, because it is a long story. However, I'll try presently to give you some idea of the contents of the oldest version which, in its present shape, may be no older than 1600 or so, although our oldest copy, as you shall hear, is half-a-century later. Before going on to the story, I must say a word about the manuscripts in which our tale is preserved.

The oldest copy which has come down is found in a MS. of 1651. It was written by a learned scribe named Dáibhí Ó Duibhgeannáin who has left us several other important MSS. The MS. is now in the Royal Irish Academy numbered 24 P 9. The *Pursuit* is the first item of a collection of tales, poems and other matter. The beginning is missing and the writing is obscured in many places; but there is little that cannot be restored with the help of other copies. Linguistically – and perhaps artistically too – this is the best text. It had been edited for the Irish Texts Society. There are several later copies dating from the eighteenth century. The oldest of them is the Royal Irish Academy MS. 23 I 27, written in 1737. Substantially this text is the same as the one edited by O'Grady. These later texts differ from the older one not only in regard to language: within the tale and at the end they contain additional matter. The most important additions are, firstly, a poem of twenty-one quatrains describing an obcurely motivated chess-game, on the authority of which some changes have been made in the text, and, secondly, a conclusion which represents Gráinne as marrying Fionn after Diarmaid's death: an ending which has strong support in tradition.

Now to give you some idea of the romance as David O'Duignan has left it to us. It was once that Fionn rose early in the morning on the Hill of Allen and sat alone on the plain without. His son Oisín and Diorraing the seer approached him and asked the reason for his early rising. He answered that a man who lacks a fitting wife is not wont to have slumber or repose. Moved to sympathy, Oisín and Diorraing undertook to arrange a marriage for Fionn with Gráinne, the daughter of Cormac the High-King. Gráinne showed no enthusiasm, but everyone else was well satisfied, and her consent was taken for granted. It was not until the great betrothal feast at Tara that she showed her hand or rather her heart, and that quite shamelessly, as you shall hear. Having caused a sleeping potion to be administered to all the assembled nobles, including her father and mother, and, of course, Fionn, but excluding a chosen few, she sat between two of the latter, Oisín and Diarmaid. Then, with rare directness, she proposed to Oisín that he should take his father's place as her husband. Unabashed by Oisín's refusal, she made a like proposal to Diarmaid, who also rebuffed her. But she was not to be denied. Without more ado, she compelled him under pain of violating solemn obligations to carry her off. Unmoved by her confession of long-standing love, the reluctant Diarmaid, after much hesitation and after taking counsel with his friends, with many a backward look, set out on the fateful adventure which, as he knew, must end in his death. *La belle dame sans merci* had him in thrall.

They went on horseback direct to Athlone where they crossed the Shannon, and leaving their horses behind them, they made their way to Doire dá Bhaoth, an imaginary wood allegedly situated in Connacht. Here Diarmaid made a clearing with seven doors, and in this clearing the lovers lay hidden. After much searching, Fionn and the Fiana reached Doire dá Bhaoth, which Diarmaid, despite previous warning of Fionn's approach, had refused to leave. Now surrounded on all sides, Diarmaid himself refuses to be rescued by his Otherworld fosterfather, Aonghus of the Brugh, who intervenes, but allows him to save Gráinne. Finally, as the result of a prodigious leap, he escapes, and follows Aonghus and Gráinne to Ros dá Roshoileach, an imaginary place identified as Limerick. From this on until we reach two-thirds of the way through the tale, Fionn and the Fiana take no direct part in the adventures of the lovers. Their adventures may be conveniently divided geographically into those which take place in the district of Sliabh Luachra in Kerry, and those which happen in Dubhros 'the black wood', a place supposed to be situated in North Connacht. I should like to tell you about their marvellous adventures, but unfortunately they do not advance the action very much.

When Diarmaid and Gráinne are in Dubhros, Fionn again takes up the chase. Diarmaid, by killing a giant named An Searbhán Lochlannach, has gained possession of a marvellous quicken-tree which bears berries having magic properties. (You will recognise immediately that Diarmaid and Gráinne are really in the Irish equivalent of the Greek Otherworld Garden of the Hesperides, and that, like Hercules, Diarmaid, at Gráinne's command, has accomplished the task of obtaining the magic fruit.) Now, Fionn attempts to bring Diarmaid to account. Gráinne and he are hiding in the magic tree, and Fionn and the Fiana are underneath it. Again Aonghus of the Brugh intervenes and rescues Gráinne, and again Diarmaid, by dint of his own prowess, eludes his enemy.

Following this incident Aonghus made peace between

the rivals. We are told that the peace lasted sixteen years and that during this time Diarmaid and Gráinne lived prosperously in Ráth Ghráinne in Keshcorran, Co. Sligo, and that she bore him four sons and a daughter. But then came the treacherous chase of the magic pig of Beann Ghulban in Co. Sligo, arranged by Fionn. Now you should know two things: first, that the pig was coeval with Diarmaid and at one time, in human form, had been his foster-brother, and, second, that arising out of the metamorphosis, it was taboo for Diarmaid ever to hunt a pig. Diarmaid slays the monster but is mortally wounded in the combat, and lies in agony when Fionn and the Fiana come upon him. Fionn has the gift of healing, but despite appeal and threat allows him to die.

There is little more to tell. The news was brought to Gráinne, who was then heavy with child. And Aonghus came and wept aloud for his fosterson, and bore away his body for burial in Brugh na Bóinne, the ancient burial-ground of Newgrange, Co. Meath. Then Gráinne summoned her children and divided their father's heritage between them, and exhorted them to avenge his death.

Thus ends the tale. You will agree, I think, that this fine story deserved treatment by a consummate master of the art of story-telling. When it was written the immediacy, the austereness, the rugged strength had gone out of Irish story-telling. Compared with the ninth century version of that great tale of elopement, the Deirdre story, *Longas mac nUisnig,* the *Pursuit,* perhaps, is not a major artistic achievement. But it is a much longer tale. Anyway, one must not compare the evening of a long tradition with the morning when

'The world-wide air was azure
And all the brooks ran gold.'

When set beside other modern tales of the Finn cycle –
tales such as *Cath Fionntrágha,* the *Bruidhean*-tales,
the *Giolla Deacair,* the *Tóraigheacht* is seen to possess
merits which mark it out as the most charming story
in modern Irish manuscript literature. In human interest it surpasses them all. Stylistically also it is a
pleasing tale. Indeed I think that in directness and sim-
plicity of language and style, and even in spirit, it is not
unworthy of comparison with the great *Acallam na
Senórach* itself.

And the tale has its moments. The opening episode
leading up to and including the elopement is well told,
and the action moves at a brisk pace down to where
Diarmaid, now become a superman under the pressure
of overwhelming odds, makes his first escape from the
implacable Fionn. Again in the narrative of Diarmaid's
death there is a power and a tension and a pathos that
grip the reader. Let me illustrate this by translating the
passage which tells how Diarmaid went forth to meet his
death:

Gráinne and Diarmaid lay asleep in Ráth Ghráinne,
and Diarmaid heard the bay of a hound through his
sleep in the night, and he started out of his sleep and
Gráinne caught hold of him and asked what he had
heard:

'I heard the bay of a hound,' he said 'and I marvel to
hear it in the night.'

'Safe keeping on thee!' said Gráinne. 'For it is the

Tuatha Dé Danann that do that to harm thee, despite Aonghus's ward over thee. And do thou lie down again in thy couch and heed it not.' Diarmaid lay down again and sleep had not fallen on him when again he heard the bay of the hound. And he stood up and Gráinne laid hold on him and said to him not to go where a hound bays in the night.

Diarmaid lay down on the couch and a deep sleep and lasting slumber fell on him, and for the third time the bay of the hound awoke him. And day in its full light came to him afterwards, and he arose and said he would go where the hound had bayed, since morning was come.

'Well then,' said Gráinne, 'take thou the Móraltach, even the sword of Manannán, and the Ga Dearg of Donn.'

'I will not,' said Diarmaid; 'I will take the Beagaltach and Ga Buidhe an Lámhaigh, and Mac an Chuill on the leash in my hand.'

Diarmaid went forth from Ráth Ghráinne and he did not stay or rest until he reached the summit of Beann Ghulban. And he found Fionn there before him quite alone, and he gave him no greeting but asked him was it he that was holding the chase.

Fionn told him that it was not he, 'But,' he said, 'a company, with which I rode out awhile since; and one of our hounds that was running loose along with us chanced to come upon a spoor of wild pig and could not be caught. And it is the boar of Beann Ghulban that he met, and it is idle for the Fiana to pursue it since often aforetime it has escaped them, and it killed fifty warriors of the Fiana this morning. And it is coming up the Peak towards us with the Fiana in flight before it, so let us leave this hillock to it.'

Diarmaid said he would not leave the hillock...

The tension following this is relaxed for a time by the telling of an in-tale; but later on it mounts again in the narrative of Diarmaid's death-agony. Now Fionn, full of malice, is deaf to Diarmaid's appeals for a drink from his healing hands; and the tale continues:

Then Oscar son of Oisín (Fionn's own grandson) spoke: 'Fionn,' said he, 'knowest thou that I am more nearly akin to thee than to Diarmaid Ó Duibhne and that I would not suffer thee to withhold a drink from him.' 'I know not a spring on this peak,' said Fionn. 'That is not true,' said Diarmaid, 'for not nine paces from thee is the finest fresh-water spring that is best in all the world.' Then Fionn went to the spring and raised the full of his two cupped hands, but he had come no more than half of the way when he let the water pass through his hands, and he said he could not bring the water. 'I pledge my word,' said Diarmaid, 'that it is of thine own will that thou dost so.' Fionn went to fetch the water again, and he had brought it no farther when he let it pass through his hands. 'I swear and my weapons are my witness,' said Oscar, 'if thou bring not the water speedily, Fionn, that only the stronger of us twain shall leave this place.' Fionn, at those words, turned for the third time to fetch the water and he brought the full of his cupped hands of it, and as he was coming forward Diarmaid's spirit parted from his body. And then says the tale 'the company of the Fiana of Ireland that was in that place raised three grievous, exceeding mighty shouts of lamentation to the skies bewailing Diarmaid Ó Duibhne.'

Apart from the question of characterization, the weakness of the *Pursuit* is in its structure. It is evident that the author had a mass of traditions to draw on, only a fraction of which now survives. How much of the traditional material was written and how much oral are questions we cannot answer. Undoubtedly, whether written or oral, the traditions for the most part were genuinely old. For example, the explanation of how it came about that Diarmaid was under a sacred obligation never to hunt a pig bears all the marks of age. On the other hand there is evidence that the author incorporated episodes which, for lack of convincing motivation, do not fit easily into the narrative. One of these is the chess-game played by Fionn and Oisín under the magic quicken-tree in which Diarmaid and Gráinne were hidden. In general, the body of the tale consists of a series of loosely knit adventures in which Fionn has no direct part. This is a major literary defect; but there may well be more to it than mere lack of skill on the part of the writer. Much more could be said about the matter and the structure of the tale, but perhaps enough has been said to suggest that it is not a simple, straightforward, late romance with an unhappy ending. It is that on the surface only.

I can deal here only very briefly with one other problem, a main one perhaps, that of interpretation. I have said already that the Ireland in which the action of the

Pursuit is imagined to have taken place is the land of Irish story-telling. In fact, we may identify it with Fairyland or the Otherworld of pagan Irish belief. Once this is recognised, most of the puzzling episodes and contradictions of the *Pursuit* cease to baffle us and essentially the tale is seen to be an imperfectly carried out romanticization of a confused tissue of mythological material. And what of the chief characters? O'Grady long ago compared Diarmaid with Adonis, the Greek god, who, as you remember, like a number of other gods, was slain by a boar. That Diarmaid originally was a deity is not open to doubt. He is to be identified with the well-known god Donn, the Lord of the pagan Irish Happy Otherworld, of whom wide-spread traditions survive. The genealogists make him the 'son of Donn, son of Donnchadh'; but this is invention. He is frequently called 'Diarmaid donn', which as I think, is only an inversion of Donn Diarmaid, meaning 'Donn the Unenvious'. His surname Ó Duibhne marks his association with the *Corcu Duibhne* the Ernean people who gave their name to Corca Dhuibne in West Kerry. Gráinne likewise is a mythical personage. Her name may mean 'the hateful goddess', which would well describe her true nature. Although there is but little trace of her real nature in the literary *Pursuit,* I think Gráinne really is the ugly goddess: the loathsome crone, who becomes a radiantly beautiful maiden when she marries the sacred King in many Irish stories of kingship. Under another name this very personage has an encounter with Diarmaid in a Scottish folktale. So the mysterious hag we met in *Leaba na Caillighe,* the name cromlechs occasionally bear, would really be Gráinne. Fionn, too, as the researches of Professor Murphy and the late Professor O'Rahilly have convincingly shown, was a divinity, probably the Otherworld God of another pagan Irish tribe. Accordingly, the *Pursuit of Diarmaid and Gráinne* may be interpreted as a romanticized development of the myth of the rivalry of two pagan divinities for possession of – what? A goddess? Lordship of the Otherworld? Lordship of this world? All of these, perhaps. It is a theme that has come out of the deep well of immemorial time in which Myth has its source. In origin it is an answer to an eternal problem posed by the groping human intellect. In its present form it is an elaboration of a half-forgotten, half-remembered thought from the treasure-trove of the Gaelic race's timeless memory.

XI

CATH MAIGE MUCCRIME

By James Carney

The fundamental theme of the Battle of Mag Muccrime is one which has been inextricably bound up with our concept of ourselves as a people, for the story both enshrines and propagates a messianic idea which in medieval times was a strong sustaining food for pride in kin and race. Nor is this concept dead. Indeed, it has such potency, is so endemic to the soil, that it could constrain a poet-mystic to recreate it in our own time as if from his own vision and to express it in terms relevant to contemporary circumstances. The poet is George Russell and I shall later quote his description of his prophetic vision. This vision could be understood by anyone with a superficial knowledge of the recent history of Ireland. The saga, on the other hand, demands knowledge of things once as familiar as the catechism, but now only reckoned significant by a handful of specialists: written in its earliest form (which is that considered here) about 800, it calls for knowledge of the dynastic position in Ireland at that date and especially of the traditional relationship of the Tara kingship to the dynastic families of Connacht and Airgialla. This saga is not so much an account of a battle as of the begetting, birth, and upbringing of Cormac, son of Art, son of Conn. It is the story, sacred if we think politically, of the beginnings of the dominance of the greatest dynastic kindred that Ireland has known, a kindred whose full powers lasted until the Norman invasion, and whose prestige was not greatly undermined until Cromwell.

This great family was originally known as the Uí Chuinn or descendants of Conn. In the fifth century, at the coming of Christianity, they controlled Tara and were at enmity with the Leinstermen, whose ancient capital Tara had been. At this time lived Niall Noígiallach, and he and Cormac are close competitors for the honour of being regarded as the most important dynastic figures which this kindred produced. Niall was king of Tara, hence the premier figure amongst those who were regarded as descendants of Conn. A generation after his death, about 484, his descendants, by winning the battle of Ocha, succeeded in bringing about a state of affairs where succession to the kingship was, for many hundreds of years, to be vested exclusively in those of the descendants of Conn who were also descendants of Niall. Hence for the highest prestige it was not sufficient to be descended from Conn: one must descend from Conn through Niall. A phenomenon witnessed constantly in Irish dynastic history had occurred: so far as the kingship of Tara was concerned the part had succeeded in consuming the whole, collateral branches were pushed aside, and the political reality was expressed by the emergence of a new kin-name, Uí Néill. While the Gaelic order lasted, precedence amongst families claiming descent from Conn never ceased to be affected by the events, or supposed events, of the fifth century. Families of the first rank, such as the O'Donnells, sprang from Niall: in the second rank were descendants of Niall's brothers such as the O'Connors; lowest in this kin – but in their own estimation so superior to families outside it like the O'Byrnes that they would regard the latter as 'base' – were the remote collaterals, the Airgialla families such as the Maguires;

their ancestors, allegedly for the crime of *fingal* or kin-slaying, had been excluded from the Tara kingship.

Before dealing with the incidents, I should like to speak of the nature of this tale. It belongs to a type which might be called 'The Birth of the Child of Destiny', and the common purpose of this type of tale is to describe how evil political and social conditions were, in the past, brought to an end by the birth of a prophesied hero. There are normally five main characters: the child of destiny, his mother and father, a king who is his enemy, and a male character, his guardian during infancy; there may also be 'helpful animals' who in some strange manner befriend the child, their dumb recognition indicating his destiny. An abstraction of this tale would run somewhat as follows: There is a king, a figure of tyranny such as the Fomorian Balor. It has been prophesied that he will be slain or deposed by his daughter's son. He guards her from men, but access is gained to her, sometimes by a supernatural being, and the hero, who hence may be semi-divine, is begotten. In political versions it is often necessary that the begetter should be the rightful claimant to the throne, but even in such cases since he is usually slain immediately, he has no more influence on the course of the story than had he been a supernatural visitant. The king tries to have the child slain, but destiny cannot be evaded, so he inevitably fails. The mother seeks some male helper to guard the child in infancy. He grows to manhood in exile and eventually succeeds in slaying or deposing the king. The evil conditions are ended: there is light where there was darkness, freedom where there was oppression, prosperity and a smiling nature instead of misery and calamity; power is in the hands of the resplendent people of the Goddess Danu instead of with the dark-visaged Fomorians; in short 'we' are in power and 'they' are in servitude.

The Battle of Mag Muccrime is one of many Irish adaptations of this pattern. Art goes to battle against Mac Con, a Munster dynast. The rival forces are to meet at Mag Muccrime and the issue at stake is the kingship of Tara: this is a challenge from without for Munster never came under Uí Chuinn or Uí Néill influence, although by a fictional courtesy involving the marriage of Eógan Mór, the ancestor of the Eóganachta, to Sadb, daughter of Conn, some form of upper-class unity was attained and the Eóganacht families could be reckoned descendants of Conn on the distaff side. Art, with a small company, goes in advance of his army and comes upon a beautiful girl, Achtán, daughter of a druid-smith, Olc by name, a wealthy land-owner with such an inordinate appetite for milk that he appears to consume the full output of his enormous herds. This peculiar feature, together with the name Olc ('Evil'), reflects the basic pattern where the father of the maiden is a figure of greed and tyranny. Art falls in love with the girl. It was prophesied that 'a great dignity' would be born of her, and the druid-smith consents to a hasty union knowing that its offspring would be kings of Ireland until doom. The following day Art was defeated and slain and Mac Con usurped the throne. Nine months later the child, Cormac, was born. One day he was stolen by a wolf-bitch and, like Romulus, the founder of Rome and the ancestor of its kings, he was suckled in her cave. He was eventually rescued by a noted hunter of north Connacht, Luigne Fer Trí, who in later versions of this tradition marries Achtán. In this version he restores Cormac to his mother, warning her that his life was in danger from the king and advising her to bring him to Fiachra Cassán of Airgialla. Achtán set out with her child and, as she crossed a mountain, wolves tried to take him but he was protected by wild horses – a duplication of the 'helpful animal' motif, already expressed in terms of a wolf-bitch.

Arriving in Airgialla, Achtán comes upon Fiachra Cassán bathing in a pool, still oppressed by sorrow for Art. She tells him her story and he embraces her and weeps over Cormac. So that the infant might not be harmed by welcoming throngs, Fiachra made for him a vessel of yew, covering it with a mantle of purple. Here Cormac grew to manhood and at the age of thirty, with his father's weapons and clothes, he set out for Tara. He showed that in justice and wisdom he was superior to Mac Con, and the usurper yielded him the throne. The coming of Cormac to Tara was the beginning of its glory.

Consideration of details gives some idea of what this story conveyed at the time of its composition. In telling of the remote origins of the contemporary ruling kindred the author used a formula which, whatever its origin, was useful for presenting the beginning or the restoration of a dynasty. He showed the glorious ancestor being protected in youth by the Connachta and the Airgialla, an expression in story form of the accepted doctrine: *Airgialla it é ata nessom d'Uib Néill aithle Connacht,* 'The Airgialla are nearest (in kinship) to the Uí Néill after the Connachta'. The Airgialla had no right to the high-kingship, the Connachta but a tenuous claim, because neither group descended from Niall. But close relationship merited that they should be presented as acquiescent benefactors of the dynasty. By making Fiachra Cassán clothe the infant in purple the author, in effect, says to the Uí Néill: 'You are of imperial blood, and it is fitting that your ancestor should have been honoured as an emperor; Tara, the seat of your kingship, is the Irish Rome.' He underlines the implied comparison by making Cormac, regarded in some way as the founder of Tara, be suckled like Romulus by a wolf-bitch. He gives the dynasty the comforting assurance that from the moment of Cormac's conception destiny had decreed that his issue should be kings of Ireland until doom. Furthermore Cormac, even to the point where he entered upon his 'public life' at the late age of thirty, is presented, consciously I would say, as a human analogy to Christ; this, together with the claim advanced elsewhere, that he was a Christian by divine inspiration, would suggest to a contemporary that the authority of his descendants had the highest supernatural sanction.

The author for certain details drew upon two preexisting traditions: that of the origin of the Uí Chuinn in Cormac and that of the Uí Néill in Niall. This becomes clear from certain genealogical considerations, and especially from the character of the men who benefited Cormac in his infancy. Fiachra Cassán was of the Airgialla and in the genealogies is reckoned fourth in descent from the child to whom he acted as guardian. Not merely does Fiachra fail to fit into the story of Cormac, but according to the general tradition the Airgialla had no existence in Cormac's time nor for long afterwards. The explanation of this contradiction is, however, suggested by the fact that Fiachra Cassán is genealogically one generation earlier than Niall: he is ideally placed to have been thought of as guardian to the infant Niall. Furthermore, Niall's epithet, though commonly explained as 'of the nine hostages', seems rather to have reference to Airgialla and to the fact that it had nine subdivisions. Niall's immediate predecessors are connected with this territory, and his son Conall Cremthainne takes his epithet from one of its subdivisions.

There are analogous peculiarities in the case of Cormac's first benefactor, Luigne Fer Trí. A few corrupt Latin sentences which have survived in the Connacht genealogies give evidence of an earlier form of the tradition. Here the hero is not Cormac but an individual called Nia Noí nGrainde, or rather, since the last word seems to be corrupt, Nia Novem Generum (he is given as named from his connection with *novem genera*): all the surrounding circumstances suggest that in some way we have here a tradition of Niall. Nia was begotten in Meath, but his mother, in typical fashion, was forced to fly with the unborn child in her womb. She sought refuge in north Connacht in the territory called Luigne Fer Trí or Corcurtrí (< Corcu Fer Trí), now the barony of Leyney in Sligo. From this we learn how Luigne Fer Trí originated: this was not a man but a people called Luigne, the epithet Fer Trí, 'belonging to the Fir Trí', distinguishing them from the Luigne whose name survives in the barony of Lune, Co. Westmeath; what had been a territorial-population name has been converted into a character in legend. It is also to be noted that the surviving traditions concerning on the one hand the birth of Niall and on the other that of Nia, purport to explain the same fact: how Connacht came to be a dependency of Tara.

This saga, then, does not, as has been held by Murphy (*Saga and Myth*, 49) belong to a class of 'imperfect manuscript recordings by a man of learning of tales, which often probably, in their living oral forms, whiled away the evening for audiences gathered round the fire of a royal residence on winter nights in the seventh century'. It belongs rather to a *genre* that one might call 'political scripture', a mixture of genuine history with symbolic fiction: its function is to propagandise rather than to entertain.

It was inevitable that this saga, together with others of a similar nature, should have an effect upon Irish thought. Looking backwards the poets and historians of medieval times were made conscious of the fact that in the past intolerable conditions were frequently brought to an end by the birth of a prophesied hero. To these traditionalists it cannot but have seemed shameful that the power which once belonged to the descendants of Niall was now vested in a king who ruled from London. It was natural that they should see in this something analogous to the conditions which existed under Balor or Mac Con. It was equally natural that they should begin to look forward to the birth of a child of destiny who would restore the glory and power of the Uí Néill. This child was prophesied and would rule, it was thought, under the name Aodh Eanghach.

The earliest reference to him seems to be that in the middle Irish prophetic poem ascribed to St. Bearchán (ZCP xviii, 29–30). Here he is described as *crobhdhearg*, 'having a red hand', the reference most likely being to the bloodshed that will precede the glory of the messianic era. The thirteenth century poet Giolla Brighde Mac Con Midhe echoes this prophecy when he contemplates the red hand of Cathal Crobhdhearg Ó Conchobhair († 1224):

Táinic an Crobhdhearg go Cruachain,
an comhartha ad-chíu 'na láimh,

'The Red-handed One has come to Cruachain, I see the sign in his hand.'

An entry in the Annals of Ulster for 1214 bears further testimony to messianic hopes: *Isin bliadhain [si] dobi in t-Aedh breicci frisa raitea an Cabharthach,* 'In this year the false Aodh who was called "The Helper".' This is plainly a reference to some individual whose claims to be the 'deliverer' or 'helper' were regarded by the annalist as false.

From this period on references to Aodh Eanghach are common in professional verse. In the wars of 1592-1601 the situation on the Irish side was dominated by a triumvirate of Aodhs, or to use the conventional anglicisation, Hughs: Hugh O'Neill, Red Hugh O'Donnell, and Hugh Maguire. Prophecies gathered especially about Red Hugh, and even the authorities in Dublin Castle took note of them. When Hugh Maguire was killed in 1600 his poet Eochaidh Ó hEóghusa made a comparison which should be noted in any study of the messianic theme in Ireland. Hugh, he said, was like the pelican who feeds its brood with its own blood – his blood will be a reviving draught for the descendants of Conn. The pelican is a medieval symbol for Christ or the Eucharist, so we have here an implied comparison of Hugh Maguire with Christ, and the first nationalistic expression of the idea of the saving of the nation through a blood-sacrifice.

The last appearance of Aodh Eanghach in Ireland (though by no means the last messianic figure) was in the person of Aodh Balldearg Ó Domhnaill, Hugh

O'Donnell of the Red Mark, who came from Spain during the Williamite wars.* It is clear from the career of Red Hugh or of Balldearg that the belief in Aodh Eanghach was no mere poetic conceit. This is also made clear by an entry in the Annals of Connacht for 1537. In that year Aodh Ó Domhnaill died, and the entry shows that the annalist had believed in the prophecy and that its fulfilment was imminent in his person. Ó Domhnaill, the annalist tells us, came nearer to the kingship of Ireland than any of the posterity of Niall to whom that dignity is not reckoned: 'Moreover it was thought and widely believed, according to the likely signs that appeared in him and in the times, that he was that Aodh Eanghach whose coming late in time the prophets and seers and great learned saints of Ireland had promised.'

But these hopes were disappointed and the annalist sinks into scepticism: 'And now since it was not he, I do not believe he will ever come till the imminence of doom and the end of the world.'

The reference to the likely signs in the times adverts to the obvious fact that at certain periods a nation's pulse beats faster. There is a release of creative energy, and if status vis-a-vis another nation is not all that it should be, it is inevitable that a considerable amount of that energy will be directed towards adjusting the position. Ireland began to experience such a period before the turn of the century, and it is not unnatural that hopes should be expressed in a messianic pattern.

Pearse in his play *The King* expressed the idea in terms of an old and a young king. The old king has been sinful and God has denied his people victory. A sinless boy is made king. His arms are victorious; he is slain,

* For an account of his career see Haverty, *History of Ireland.*

but by his death his people are redeemed. The king who fails in a just war because of personal sinfulness may well be Parnell; the sinless youth who will save his people through sacrifice undoubtedly embodies Pearse's own messianic resolve. For he constantly shows that he thought of himself as a nationalistic analogy to Christ. This idea is presented most clearly in *The Singer;* speaking in the person of Mac Dara, Pearse, the messiah, has written of his life, his intention, and his passion:

'When my mother stood up to meet me with her arms stretched out to me, I thought of Mary meeting her Son on the Dolorous Way... I seemed to see myself brought to die before a great crowd that stood cold and silent; and there were some that cursed me in their hearts for having brought death into their houses... The true teacher must suffer and do: he must go into Gethsemane and toil up the steep of Golgotha... The fifteen were too many. Old men, you did not do your work well enough. You should have kept all back but one. One man can free a people as one Man redeemed the world. I will take no pike, I will go into battle with bare hands. I will stand up before the Gall as Christ hung naked before men on the tree.'

While Pearse was casting himself in a messianic rôle, a part which he played to the logical, foreseen, and desired end, Russell had assumed the rough mantle of the Baptist. One of his visions, that which I have mentioned, bears a remarkable similarity to the pattern of the story of the child of destiny. That Russell should have such a vision, and believe in it, is a phenomenon that should give us a sympathetic understanding of much in early Irish literature that we might otherwise dismiss impatiently. Sometime about 1898 his meditation was broken by a series of pictures that flashed before him with the swiftness of moving pictures. In this meditation he saw 'a vast figure aureoled with light' which assumed human shape and looked at him, a face like that of the young Napoleon. This picture was replaced by that of a woman with a blue cloak who took a child upon her lap, and from all Ireland rays of light converged upon the child. Then upon the coronation stone at Westminster he saw a figure of empire which grew weary, let fall the sceptre, and toppled from the seat. A gigantic figure, beating a drum stalked up and down, and wherever its feet fell there were sparks, swirling of flame and black smoke upward as from burning cities.

Russell's interpretation of this dream was 'that some child of destiny, around whom the future of Ireland was to pivot, was born then or to be born'. His belief was as great as that of an annalist of 1537: 'I look everywhere', he says, 'in the aspect of every new notability, hoping before I die to recognise the broad-browed avatar of my vision.'

The deliverer theme, which tends to appear wherever one nation exerts power over another, must be seen in an international perspective. In China in the last century, the Taiping rebellion against the alien Manchus was inspired by the visionary Hong-siu-tsuen who, influenced by Methodism, declared himself Son of God, brother of Christ. In the Sudan, Mahommed Ahmed revolted against the Egyptians, claiming to be a Mahdi, a divinely appointed leader. In Germany in our own day, Hitler took on a messianic character; in 1937 a German lady, a parson's widow, spoke to me of him in such terms that in defence of her orthodoxy she had to deny belief in his divinity: 'Ich meine nicht dass er Gott ist, aber er ist ein Mann von Gott gesandt.'

Amongst the British the return of Arthur was to herald the annihilation of the Saxons. In Wales, from the fourteenth century, the expected deliverer was Owain Lawgoch ('of the Red Hand'), prophesied by Y Bergam; he is identical with the red-handed Irish Aodh Eanghach prophesied by Bearchán. The deliverer idea, even when associated with particular dynasties, implies a realisation of nationhood, an idealistic conception of the antithesis of Briton and Saxon, Gael and Gall, that is not belied by disunion and dubious alliances of expediency.

It might be held (but hardly with complete justification) that the messianic thinking of Pearse, Russell, Lady Gregory, and others, was a new fashioning of the idea, having at most an academic, artificial connection with the messianism I have called endemic. However that may be, I will mention some messianic ideas still current, or current within living memory. The expected return of Aodh Balldearg Ó Domhnaill is recorded in Donegal folk-tradition; in the notes to her messianic play *The Deliverer* (1911) Lady Gregory refers to the folk-belief in the return of Parnell. About 1927 I heard advanced as an argument for supporting one political leader rather than another an old prophecy that a Spaniard would free Ireland; reference to the files of the Irish Folklore Commission in later years showed that this was no *ad hoc* prophecy invented for the occasion. It is rather, I would say, a development of the idea of Míl of Spain: what happened will happen once more; Míl will come again to succour his blood-kin. The idea that a youth of mysterious birth will free Ireland is incorporated in a commonplace 'Otherworld Mistress' tale collected in Donegal (Béaloideas, xxiii, 166). The prophecy of his return is made by the youth's Otherworld mother to his mortal father: 'You'll not see me or your son ever again until the day of the great battle between the Irish and the English; and when my son goes riding through the crowd on this black mare, on that day the battle will go with the Irish.'

The idea is here presented in a form which students of the earlier literature might regard as degenerate; but it is a recognisable current derivative of the tradition that produced birth-stories such as The Battle of Mag Muccrime and the medieval belief in Aodh Eanghach and Owain Lawgoch as deliverers of Ireland and of Wales.

XII

FINGAL RÓNÁIN

By David Greene

'How Rónán killed his son' – that's the best I can do in the way of a translation of the title of this story. The Irish has simply *Fionghal Rónáin,* and *fionghal* is really a technical term; it is the legal word for the killing of a kinsman. That, of course, was the most dreadful of crimes, for it was the duty of a murdered man's kin to exact either vengeance or compensation from the killer; but if the murderer himself belonged to the kin, human justice faltered – how much more so when the murderer was the father of the victim, and a king!

Most of the stories you have heard in this series, no matter how late they may be in respect of composition, contain very old material; you will remember, for example, that in 'the Pursuit of Diarmaid and Gráinne', which turns up only in modern Irish, we can glimpse behind the figures of Diarmaid and Fionn the same old gods who take the shape of bulls in the *Táin.* We find nothing like this in the story of Rónán and his son; no gods, no enchantments, no tabus – nothing but the everyday human ingredients of love and jealousy and hate and violence. And yet it would be hard to place this story much later than the end of the Old Irish period; so we see that, to some extent at least, the idea of pure literature, the story for the story's sake, had developed in the three centuries or so since the old oral tradition came to terms with the new Latin learning. The only trace of archaism in the story is that it is completely pagan both in spirit and expression; the author has made a half-hearted attempt to anchor it in history somewhere in the seventh century, but we cannot identify any of the characters satisfactorily from the annals. In fact, it is as little rooted in time as a Yeats verse play.

The theme is one of the oldest in the world: an ageing widower marries a young girl, who soon falls in love with her handsome step-son. She pursues him but he repulses her; her love turns to hate and she accuses him of attempting her honour. The old king, blinded with jealousy, has his son killed; he finds out, too late, how he has been tricked, and he dies of grief, while his wife dies by her own hand. It is, of course, the classical theme of Phaedra and Hippolytus, which Racine in turn used in one of his greatest plays – and, indeed, the immortal line

C'est Vénus toute entière à sa proie attachée

is a perfect summing up of the woman in the Irish story. The German scholar, Kuno Meyer, who was the first to publish *Fionghal Rónáin*, was quite convinced that it, too, was a re-working of the Greek story. I'm not at all convinced of that; I see no necessity to search for historical parallels for so simple and straightforward a plot, which might suggest itself to any writer at any time – I don't think that in T. C. Murray's *Autumn Fire*, for example, which deals with the same situation in a modern Irish setting, we need go looking for Greek origins.

The structure of the story is simple, prose at the beginning, intermingled with verse as the tension increases, and ending with a long lamentation by the king over the body of his dead son. I will summarise the first hundred lines or so, and then translate the rest of the story as literally as possible.

Rónán king of the Leinstermen, had been without a wife for many years; his son by his first wife, Mael Fhothartaigh, was the desire of all the girls and the lover of all the women. Rónán decided to marry the daughter of Eochaidh, king of Dunseverick – we never find out her name – and, against Mael Fhothartaigh's advice that he should think of a settled woman rather than of a skittish girl, he went north and married her. Mael Fhothartaigh left the court and went on a royal circuit, but the queen insisted that he should be brought back, and he promised her all loyalty and devotion for Rónán's sake. But the queen sent a beautiful maidservant to him, telling her to use every wile to procure Mael Fhothartaigh for her and threatening her with death if she failed. The girl broke down and told Mael Fhothartaigh the whole story, and he went to Scotland to avoid the danger, where he won a great reputation as a hunter and warrior. But the Leinstermen insisted that he should return. When he reached Dunseverick on the way back, the queen's father told him that he, not the old man, should have married her. But he rejected this with horror, and returned to Leinster, where the unfortunate maidservant was sent once more to assail him. In despair he consulted his fosterbrother Conghal, who offered to get rid of the woman – but for a heavy price: no less than his two hunting dogs, Daoilín and Daithlenn. Mael Fhothartaigh agreed, and Conghal told him to make a tryst with the queen at a spot called the Cows of Aoife, so-called from stones which looked like white cows at a distance. This was done and the queen eagerly kept the tryst, but was met on the way by Conghal, who reproached her for wandering about by herself and brought her home. Three times she tried to reach the spot, and each time Conghal headed her off, using a horsewhip on her the third time. She went back threatening his life – and now I go over to the words of the story:

Rónán comes home. Mael Fhothartaigh's people come in, while he remains outside hunting by himself. 'Where is Mael Fhothartaigh to-night, Conghal?,' said Rónán. 'He is out,' said Conghal. 'Alas that my son, who gives wealth to so many, should be out hunting by himself.' 'You have us deafened,' said she, 'praising your son.' 'It's right to praise him', said Rónán, 'for there is no son in Ireland who serves his father better than he. He is equally concerned, about men and women, in Dublin or in the south or the west, as concerned on my behalf as though it was his own honour were involved, so that you and I may take our ease, woman.'

'He hasn't got yet from me,' she said, 'the ease which he desires – to sleep with me in despite of you. I cannot keep holding him off any longer; Conghal brought me to him three times to-day and I barely escaped his hands.' 'A curse on your lips, you evil woman,' said Rónán, 'it is a lie.' 'You will see a token of it now,' said she; 'I'll make a half-verse, to see if what he says in reply fits it.' (He used to do that every night to entertain her; he would say a half-verse and she would make up the other half).

He came in and began to dry his shins in front of the fire, and Conghal beside him; his jester, Mac Glas, was at his games on the floor of the house. And he said, for it was a cold day:

'It is cold against the whirlwind
For him who herds the Cows of Aoife...'

'Do you hear that, Rónán?' said she:

'That is the vain herding
With neither cows, nor the one you love.'

'It is true, then,' said Rónán, and spoke to a warrior, Aodhán, who was beside him and said 'Aodhán, a spear into Mael Fhothartaigh, and let something from you reach Conghal too.'

Since he was sitting at the fire with his back towards them, Aodhán thrusts a spear into him so that its point pinned him to his seat. As Conghal got up, Aodhán put a spear through his heart. The jester leapt away and Aodhán threw a spear after him which ripped out his bowels. 'You've done enough to the men, Aodhán,' said Mael Fhothartaigh from where he sat. 'How well it was,' said Rónán, that you found no woman to woo but my wife!' 'That was a miserable lie that took you in, Rónán,' said the youth, 'that made you kill your only son without cause. By your honour, and by the tryst with death to which I go, I would as soon have thought of sinning with my mother as with her; she has been pestering me since I came home and Conghal took her away three times to-day to keep her away from me. Conghal did nothing to deserve his death.'

Meanwhile a raven was tugging at the jester's entrails on the forebridge; he was contorting his mouth and the serving men were laughing. Mael Fhothartaigh was ashamed and said:

Mac Glas
Gather in your bowels!
Why have you no shame?
– Louts are laughing at you.

The three died then and were brought into a house
apart. Rónán went and watched over his son for three
days and three nights.

Meanwhile Donn, Conghal's brother and Mael
Fhothartaigh's fosterbrother, went with twenty horsemen to Dunseverick and they tricked Eochaidh into
coming to the border, by asking him to come to meet
Mael Fhothartaigh who was running away with his
daughter, and they took his head and the heads of his
wife and son.

Rónán said over his son:

It is cold against the whirlwind
For him who herds the Cows of Aoife;
That is the vain herding,
With neither cows, nor the one you love.

The wind is cold
In the doorway of the warriors' house;
Those were dear warriors
Who used to shield me from the wind.

Sleep, daughter of Eochaidh,
Very sharp is the wind;
I am sad that Mael Fhothartaigh
Should die through the sin of an evil woman.

Sleep, daughter of Eochaidh,
I grieve, while you sleep,
To see Mael Fhothartaigh,
In his bloodstained shirt.

She said:

Alas, o corpse in the corner,
That many eyes looked upon,
The sin that I committed
Was to torment you after your banishment.

Rónán said:

Sleep, daughter of Eochaidh,
Men are not fools!
Though you wet your mantle
It is not my son that you lament.

Then Donn came and threw her father's head into her
bosom, and her mother's and her brother's. She rose
up then and fell on her knife so that it came through
her back. Then Rónán said:

Eochaidh has got a single shirt
After being in a long warm cloak;
The sorrow which is upon Naas
Is also on Dunseverick.

Give food, give drink,
To Mael Fhothartaigh's dog;
And let some other one give
Food to Conghal's dog.

Give food, give drink
To Mael Fhothartaigh's dog;
The dog of a man who would give food
To everybody, though he might buy it dearly.

I am sad that Daithlenn's sides
Should be beaten with sore rods;
It is not she I reproach
– She did not betray our dear ones.

Daoilín
It is she who served me;
Her head is in each man's lap in turn
Seeking one whom she has not found.

The men, the youths, the horses
Which were around Mael Fhothartaigh
– They were not anxious for anyone's protection
In the lifetime of their lord.

The men, the youths, the horses
Which were around Mael Fhothartaigh
– They used to range freely in the plain,
They used to race against each other.

The men, the youths, the horses
Which were round Mael Fhothartaigh
– Many's the time they were
With shouts of triumph after great victories.

Mael Fhothartaigh's people
– Though I do not say they were dishonoured –
Did not stand well by the man
Who relieved all their needs.

My son Mael Fhothartaigh,
Whose dwelling was the tall forest,
Neither king nor prince
Trespassed lightly on his land.

My son Mael Fhothartaigh
Who rode round sea-girt Scotland,
He was a warrior among warriors,
He held his sway over them.

My son Mael Fhothartaigh
He was the upholder of the hunting;
The tall bright shining tree
Has found a cold dwelling.

Then the Leinstermen surrounded Rónán at the keen-
ing and knocked him over. They fell on Aodhán, who
was seized by Mael Fhothartaigh's two sons, Aodh
and Maol Tuile. Aodh stabbed him until he was rid-
dled with wounds. 'Let me up, men,' said Rónán, 'unless you want to kill me. Is the man dead?' 'Dead,
indeed,' said the warriors. 'Who killed him,' said he.
'Aodh,' said the warriors. 'Did Maol Tuile strike
him?,' said Rónán. 'No,' said the warriors. 'May he
never kill anybody!' said Rónán. 'May the lad who
killed him, however, be the foremost in war and fighting.' And he said:

It is a great deed
For the son of a lout to slay the son of a king;
That was clear in his dying hour
To Aodhán, the son of Fiachna.

The fighting was carried up to him then in front of the

house. It is then he said:

> Alas that Mael Fhothartaigh is not here
> For this fighting in the plain;
> This old warrior has not the strength
> To approach the new battle.

With that a gush of blood burst over his lips and he died at once.
That is Rónán's murder of his son.

After the fine poetry of Rónán's lament, the ending may seem to some of you to be a little clumsily contrived. And yet I think we can see how natural it was to its audience that the Leinstermen, after respecting the king's mourning for three whole days, should finally break in to avenge their hero and, sweeping the king aside, seize the murderer. You'll notice that the avenger is said to be one of Mael Fhothartaigh's sons – no doubt by one of his many loves – though it should be said that another version gives the task to the fosterbrother who has already taken the heads of the queen's father and mother. And the old king dies then, before the maddened Leinstermen can complete their vengeance by laying hands on their own king.

So much for the story which was, I think, a good one to choose to end our survey of early Irish saga. As I said in the beginning, we have come a long way from the origin-tales and law-texts, from the gods transformed into bulls and men, and from the stories of the birth of miraculous children. Leaving aside the poems, we could imagine ourselves in the world of Icelandic saga, that prose literature which, of all medieval story-telling, has made most impression on modern readers by its bare, witty language and its plain straightforward narratives. I myself do not think that this is an accident; still less would I suggest that our story had been influenced by Scandinavian literature, although it must have been composed well after the beginning of their raids on Ireland. No, I hold the view that the debt is in the other direction, and that it was in Ireland that the barbarous Norsemen first came into contact with a cultivated literature. It seems impossible to me to overlook the resemblances between early Icelandic poetry, with its elaborate schemes of rhymes and alliterations, and the early Irish and Welsh systems, which go back to the fusion of Latin learning with the native oral tradition. Our task is more difficult with prose, precisely because the saga material has been so much better preserved than have our own stories, and still the coincidence that the Scandinavians, who had no old prose literature of their own, were at the critical period in such close touch with an Ireland that had succeeded in bringing what we may call the short story to such a height of perfection – that coincidence is too striking to be ignored.

But why have we so little of it left in Ireland? Furthermore, why does the Irish tradition, so to speak, relapse into the older taste at a later period? Why do compositions which are obviously later than *Fionghal Rónáin* – *Agallamh na Seanórach* and *Diarmuid agus Gráinne,* for example, simply work over the old tales and the old beliefs, instead of consolidating the ground won by this new attitude to story-telling? No complete answer to these questions can be given, but a glance at the historical background may help us to understand what happened.

When I was talking about the *Táin,* I said that we

must date the beginning of written Irish, and therefore of Irish literature in the real sense of the word, to the period from the beginning of the seventh century onwards, when the keepers of the old tradition came to terms with the Church and with Latin writing. It was not only the poets who had changed their outlook; the clergy of the seventh century were no longer hermits, but were beginning to build up their communities into monastic towns – the only towns Ireland knew until the Scandinavians came – where literature and the arts were cultivated. It is no accident that the golden age both of Irish art and Irish literature should be to all intents and purposes the same, and that both should begin to decline at the same period.

That decline begins in the ninth century; in the words of Mlle. Henry, speaking of the art of the period: 'The upheaval brought about by the Scandinavian invasions on one hand, the attraction of continental models – first Carolingian, then Roman – on the other, contribute to destroy the fragile combination of circumstances which had permitted its growth and determined its originality. The illuminators, fleeing before the invasion, emigrate to the continent.' You will notice that Mlle. Henry does not say that the monks in general fled to the Continent; no, it was the artists who went, leaving their more spiritually minded brethren behind them to face the new circumstances. The same process may be noted on the intellectual side; as has often been remarked, the Irish monks in Europe at this period are scholars rather than spiritual leaders. There seems to be little doubt that this draining off of the more worldly elements, combined perhaps with a belief that the sufferings inflicted by the heathen raiders were a judgment on a luxury-loving society, helped on a puritan reaction in the Irish Church – a reaction which had already begun in the eighth century with such leaders as St. Mael Ruain of Tallaght.

Under the conditions, literature was bound to become suspect. Writing in Irish continued, of course, for the vernacular was too well established as the ordinary language for pious and devotional works for any change to be possible – in any case, asceticism and polished Latinity were unlikely to go together. But works of pure entertainment can hardly have been encouraged, nor were literary men likely to find much hospitality in a war-torn country. It is hardly surprising that not one single manuscript in Old Irish is preserved in this country, while on the continent we find at least a few poems interspersed amongst more arid material. It may well be that we should associate the sudden breakdown of the language we know as Old Irish with these circumstances; just as intense literary cultivation favours conservatism in language, so a slackening allows the speech of the common people to take over - we have a very good parallel in the sudden coming to light of Scottish Gaelic and the modern Irish dialects once the bardic system and bardic language broke down in the seventeenth century. It does not appear that the cultivation of secular Irish literature became really popular again until the twelfth century, when the great collections which we know as Leabhar na hUidhre and the Book of Leinster were compiled – together, no doubt, with many others now lost. A great pa.t of these compilations is devoted to what can only be called antiquarianism – to the indiscriminate recovery of old traditions. A further step was the refurbishing of these traditions, the attempt to arrange them in more coherent form; as I remarked when talking on the *Táin,* the Leabhar na hUidhre version and that of the Book of Leinster represent those two tendencies. But, even in the Book of Leinster *Táin,* that is, the modernising version, we find a terrible amount of deliberate archaising, a stifling weight of dead matter. More and more, Irish prose literature becomes the preserve of antiquarians, while the poets devote themselves increasingly to the elaboration of praise poetry. I hope I will not be thought fanciful if I say that much of later Irish literature reminds me of modern exercises in what we call 'Celtic illumination'; the artists have studied their sources, they possess considerable skill, they devote themselves wholeheartedly to their work, but somehow the vitality is missing and we feel that the work does not speak to the condition of the modern man. Old Irish literature had achieved the difficult synthesis between tradition and learning and, still more important, had shown a real creative spirit; after that strange crisis, later Irish literature rests almost wholly on tradition. When the Renaissance was lighting up men's imaginations throughout Europe, Irish literary men were working over the Pursuit of Diarmaid and Gráinne.

MORE MERCIER BESTSELLERS

'THAT'S HOW IT WAS'
Kevin Danaher.

Irish folk tradition is a wonderful mixture of fact and fancy. Many people believe that our forefathers were so simple and credulous that they believed everything they heard. This is not true and although there were people who would swallow any tall story just as there are many people today who believe every word in television advertisments the average person long ago knew the difference between the fact and fiction that abounded in folk tradition.

Stories believed to be true, especially tales of past happenings were always certified by the saying 'That's how it was', indicating that the **seanchai** believed it and you had better believe it too, at least within his hearing !

With Kevin Danaher we travel the roads with the farmers and drovers on the way to the fairs and we meet the **spailpins** tramps, tinkers and the travelling musicians and listen to them swap greetings and gossip. We travel the roads our forefathers walked, we rest under the trees that shaded them and we pass the walls that heard their songs and laughter.

IRISH LIFE AND LORE
Seamus O Cathain

Irish Life and Lore is not only an excellent collection of folktales and legends but it is also packed with the lore and traditions of places and people from the four corners of Ireland.

This book contains much new material which was never published before and which is drawn from the manuscript archive of the former Irish Folklore Commission, now the Department of Irish Folklore at University College, Dublin and also from the living Irish folk tradition of today.

Irish Life and Lore includes authentic folk material culled from nineteenth century writers such as Kennedy and Crofton Croker and also from the author's own extensive field collections made in various parts of the country.